THE CIA GUIDE TO CLANDESTINE OPERATIONS

Varangian Press

The CIA Guide to Clandestine Operations

copyright © Varangian Enterprises 2011

Varangian Press
All Rights Reserved

Cover Design by Varangian Press

Varangian Press is a trademark of Varangian Enterprises, Denver Colorado 80250

ISBN: 978146362-715-7

Printed in the United States of America

THE CIA GUIDE TO CLANDESTINE OPERATIONS

2011

VARANGIAN PRESS

Contents

Table of Contents

Table of Contents

Table of Contents

Table of Contents

PREFACE

CIA Global Liaison and Training Operations

Since the early 1970's, the CIA has, for various reasons, became a very risk adverse organization. Clandestine operations by their very nature are high risk ventures. One solution to the CIA's problem was to enter in to joint clandestine ventures with foreign governments whose intelligence agencies were known for their professionalism and expertise. The CIA financed these ventures and their partner ran the operation and assumed the risk. The CIA shared in any intelligence produced in these operations. Great Britain's MI6 and Israel's Mossad were frequent partners in these types of clandestine operations.

The second solution was to train and liaison with lesser foreign intelligence agencies. Many times the funding for this training was concealed in Foreign Aid packages. This type of relationship allowed the CIA to maintain a "Big Brother" relationship with certain foreign intelligence agencies for years. The parameters of this relationship allowed the CIA to utilize the "Little Brother's" resources and manpower to collect intelligence on common enemies, such as the Soviet Union.

Preface

The CIA's training materials formed the basis or in some cases, the entirety of the host countries doctrine. Much of the third world's intelligence agencies in Asia, South America, the Middle East, and Africa owe their clandestine tradecraft to the CIA. This guide was written from instructional materials provided by the CIA to an intelligence agency of one the key allies of America's Global War on Terror and is still current doctrine.

The means and methods of Technical Surveillance and Technical Counter Surveillance are notably absent from this manual. These collection disciplines are dependent upon technologies that are continually reviewed and revised. For this reason technical collection is a specialized clandestine skill set and therefore beyond the scope of this manual.

INTRODUCTION

THE INTELLIGENCE CYCLE

Intelligence Cycle

The Intelligence Cycle is a step by step process by which information is assembled and converted to intelligence and made available to the user through the phases of planning and directing the collection effort, collection, processing, and dissemination and use.

Planning and Directing Intelligence Collection

Once a mission is received, the Intelligence Officer reevaluates the intelligence he has on hand and recommends what additional intelligence is needed by the Commander for planning and making decisions. This is referred to as the Intelligence Estimate, which is about the enemy and the terrain, also known as Basic Intelligence. The need to reevaluate this Basic Intelligence formulates other intelligence requirements, which serves as the basis for the collection of Current Intelligence. Intelligence planning begins before the planning of other staff functions. Until an Intelligence Estimate is available, detailed operational planning cannot be completed. The intelligence officer must be ready to provide an estimate for the next operation and revise the current estimate to meet changed operational conditions. The five steps in intelligence planning are; determine the intelligence required for operations and plans, determine the priority (PIR and OIR) of need for each of the different items, determine those enemy activity or characteristics of the area or operations which would affect the answer to the intelligence requirements, determine the specific items of information the presence or absence of would affect or refute pertinent indications, select collection agencies and prepare and dispatch appropriate orders, and supervise the collection effort through staff visits, review of records, reports and inspections to insure productive and timely collection of information.

Collection phase of the Intelligence Cycle

The collection phase is the most dangerous phase of the Intelligence Cycle which concerns the gathering of information through sources such as; people, paid informants, defectors, captured insurgents, aerial photos and electronic data. This phase is a systematic exploitation of the sources available by the collecting agencies and the delivery of information obtained to the intelligence section.

The Collection Plan is the product of the Planning Phase. This plan is a continually changing, working model in the collection of information. It assists the intelligence officer in the coordination and collection efforts of the collecting agencies and in keeping all elements of the intelligence structure informed of collection activities. Collection plans are not made up in any prescribed form. It can range from a fragmentary worksheet to a detailed plan or it may be a mental plan alone. The type and make up of the collection plan will vary upon the size of the unit, the mission, the situation, and the personalities concerned. The following items contained in the collection plan are; PIR and OIR, indications pertinent to PIR and OIR, specific information required (SIR) in connection with each indication, agencies to be used to obtain the required information, place and time the information is to be reported, and a column to indicate progress of the collection effort and notes for further action.

Human Intelligence Collectors that are often used in collection plans are:

- Physical Surveillance Teams
- Technical Surveillance Teams
- Undercover Teams
- Interrogation Teams
- Counterintelligence Investigators
- Agent Operations

The Human Source Collection Plan makes use of the following types of Sources:

Incidental Informant

-Incidental informants are individuals who provide information with no intention of repeating this service or furnishing information on a continuing basis.

Unwitting Informants

-Unwitting informants are individuals who provide information of intelligence value with being aware they are imparting such information. Information may be obtained from these persons through elicitation or by technical surveillance.

Casual Informants

-A casual informant is one who by professional or social position as access to information of continuing interest and provides this information willingly either through specific request or voluntarily. A Casual Informant is under no obligation to furnish information and under so much control as he is willing to accept. Casual Informants are willing to furnish what information he routinely has available with no assurance that he would not share the same information with any other agency. Walk-ins, Call-ins, and Write-ins are types of Casual Informants.

Official Informants

-Official Informants are those individuals who by virtue of their office are obligated to furnish information to intelligence agencies in the normal course of their duties. Certain police officers, government officials, and technical experts are examples of Official Informants. Continuing contact with Official Agents over a period of time will frequently result in a relationship where the degree of cooperation with the intelligence unit and the amount of information provided extends far beyond what is inherent in the official position. In such cases the Official Informant maybe developed into a recruited agent.

Trusted Informants

-Informants with a history of furnishing accurate information over a period of time are deemed to be trusted informants and are considered for agent development. These informants must report accurately over three separate occasions and a Basic Source Data report must be submitted for background investigation to meet this criteria.

Directed Informants

-Directed Informants are individuals who accept direction from Intelligence personnel as Guides or Target Designators. Informants who report accurate information over a period of time are judged to have both placement and access. These informants should be persuaded to take on the role of either Guides or Designators. Successful guides and designators prove ability to accept control and are considered for Recruitment.

RECRUITED AGENTS-

Agent

- a person who is aware that he is engaged in a clandestine activity on behalf of a sponsor and who submits to some degree of control by the clandestine organization.

Access Agents- are native personnel who have access to population groups with access to required information.

Introduction

Recruited Informants/Action Agents

-Informants are individuals who obtain the required information during the course of their normal daily activities. They are distinguished from casual informants because they submit to operational control. Informant/Action Agents, sometimes known as Low Level Sources, are primarily used for area intelligence. Hotel and restaurant personnel, merchants in bazaars, traveling businessmen are examples of Recruited informants.

Principal Agent

- an intelligence agent who has developed his information net within a

target group or in a particular area of operations.

Resident Agent

-is a term for an agent who is the resident of a third country while performing the duties of an Agent Handler for operations in the target country.

Action Agent

– a term used in Agent Acquisition, which refers to a recruited and documented intelligence agent with access and or placement to a threat group.

Penetration Agent-a term used in Agent Acquisition, which refers to a recruited and documented agent with placement and access in a threat group. They may be recruited outside the target and placed therein or more usually recruited from personnel within the target itself. Penetration Agents are particularly vulnerable to detection and must receive intensive security instruction to prevent their compromise.

Site Agent

– in Agent Acquisition, an agent in-charge of the security survey and security measures at a certain location to be visited by the principal.

Support Agent

- a person who extends assistance to the intelligence operations.

Human Sources and operational techniques available to satisfy collection requirements:
Incidental Sources

- Individuals who furnish information with no intention of offering their services again.
  - Travelers
  - Refugees
  - Border crossers
  - Deserters
  - P.O.W.s
  - Detainees
  - Local residents
  - Anonymous tipsters
  - Escapees/returnees
- Contacted through:

Introduction

- o Cordon and search
- o Patrols
- o Checkpoints
- o Entry screening
- o House to house searches
- o Surveys
- o Suggestion boxes
- o Hot lines/Tip lines
- o POW/Prison screening and interrogation
- o Rendition/rescue ops
- Information usually gained by interrogation/interviewing methods
  - o Learn of enemy weaknesses
  - o Damage assessment, casualty assessment
  - o Obtain personality information about FIS personnel
  - o Detect/Identify/locate insurgent, special operations, espionage personnel
  - o Identify recruitment attempts by FIS
  - o Learn of other defectors/collaborators working with enemy
  - o Gain information about prisoners/MIA/KIA
  - o Determine MO regarding enemy prisoner handling, interrogation
  - o Impending terrorist/insurgent operations
  - o Enemy OB intelligence
  - o Arms/supply caches
  - o G base locations
  - o Infiltration routes

- o Local social, economic, political conditions

Unwitting Sources

- Individuals who impart information without knowing that they are doing so.
  - o Subject experts
  - o Retired military, technical, scientific, political leaders or subject experts
  - o Politicians
  - o Hostile military liaison officers
  - o Scientific experts
  - o Technical experts
  - o Academics
  - o Corporate officers
  - o Busy bodies
  - o Also most types found under informant entry
- Information usually gained by:
  - o Elicitation
  - o Eavesdropping conversations
  - o Observation
  - o Surveillance
  - o Surreptitious entry
  - o Technical surveillance

Introduction

Casual Sources

- Individuals by benefit of social or professional position possess or have access to information on a continual basis
    - Prominent citizens
    - Retired law enforcement, military, political, or business leaders
    - Members of NGO's
    - Walk ins
- Willing to impart this information either on request or by his own initiative
- Casual agents are under no obligation to furnish information
- Subject only to as much control as they are willing to accept
- Usually willing to supply only the information that is routinely available to them
- Information usually gained by mixture of interview and elicitation methods

Official Sources

- Individuals by reason of their professional obligations are expected or required to give information to intelligence agencies during the normal course of their duties
    - Government officials
    - Police and security officers
    - Technical experts
- Information gained through liaison/elicitation
    - Investigative
    - Operational

o   Threat

- Continued liaison may result in cooperation beyond official responsibilities

- If this does happen, sometimes may be developed into recruited agents

Processing of Information phase of the Intelligence Cycle

This is the step in the intelligence cycle where the information collected is converted into intelligence. Information is processed as received without waiting to collect additional information. The intelligence derived from fragmentary information may be particularly essential to targeting or rapidly changing situations. If time permits, a search is directed for additional information to complete, confirm, or refute the intelligence developed from fragmentary information. The three steps in processing are; recording, evaluation, and interpretation. The sequence in procession depends upon the nature and urgency of the information. Recording is usually the first step; however, on urgent items, recording may occur simultaneously with evaluation and interpretation. Information needed immediately by higher, lower or requesting units may be disseminated before it is completely processed.

Dissemination and use of Intelligence and Information

This is a phase of the Intelligence Cycle which defines the timely conveyance of information or intelligence in an appropriate form and any suitable means to those who need it. The primary purpose of timely dissemination of intelligence is to enable the commander to make a decision with confidence; a secondary purpose is to provide knowledge in the light of which new information may be processed. Intelligence is used in much the same manner at all echelons. The means of dissemination are like wise similar at all echelons, with variations occurring in the volume, frequency, and coverage. Personal contact, briefings, and distribution of intelligence estimates, analyses of the area of operations, and written reports usually make dissemination.

THE INTELLIGENCE OPERATION CYCLE

Operational Cycle

The Operational Cycle is the chronological development of intelligence activities from receipt of the basic requirement to the final product-the Intelligence Report. It is called a cycle, for one reason only; to emphasize that intelligence activities are never a completed action but rather a cycle of evolutionary developments. The operational cycle should not be considered as a "cure-all" procedure that will give answers to all our questions or problems, which might arise. Let us consider the operational cycle purely as a series of guidelines, which will assist us in both planning operation, and in conducting them in a systematic, methodical and efficient maneuver. There are two basic elements which must be considered and which should be present in every operational cycle. These are: Every intelligence action, that is, every operational cycle, is set in motion by the assignment of a mission or target; and every operational cycle, that is, every intelligence operational cycle, is made up of three component parts, the target or mission, the agent or agents, and the support facilities and functions.

Generally speaking, the Operational Cycle is utilized only when there is no other way to satisfy the requirement but to recruit an informer or agent with access to the target. This maybe the case with closed targets where much of the collected All Source Intelligence is judged to be propaganda, disinformation, and misinformation designed to deceive as to the target's intentions.

Introduction

Part 1

Undercover Operations

CHAPTER 1: UNDERCOVER OPERATIONS

Undercover Operations

Undercover Operations are an investigative technique in which the investigator conceals his true identity and status and adopt an assume role in order to obtain access to information and evidence which would not be available to other investigative means. It maybe employed in all types of investigation but it must be applicable in operations to design to counter hostile espionage, sabotage and subversive activities. Undercover maybe used directly by special agencies, or indirectly, by controlled informants acting under the direction of counterintelligence personnel. Undercover Operations are utilized to:

- Collect Target Study intelligence
- Collect Target Area intelligence
- Monitor organizations, locations, or individuals for indications of
  - Espionage
  - Sabotage
  - Subversive activities
- Conduct deniable
  - Elicitation interviews

       o   Interrogations

- Investigate Source groups to spot potential agents
- Investigate and Assess potential agents
- Recruit Agents
- Operate as Agent Handler

An Undercover Story is a biographical account true or fictional or combination of both, which portrays the undercover investigator past, history, and current status. The undercover story allows the operative to penetrate the target organization or area, geographical area or physical location where the intelligence operation is carried out.

Undercover operations are of two main types: Long Range Undercover Operations and Short Range Undercover Operations.

Long range undercover operation is a type of undercover operation which provides reliable, accurate, and continuing access to information, which would not otherwise be attainable; However, its extensive use is limited by the need for careful preparation, which requires considerable time and effort before it can be expected to produce any worthwhile results. It requires painstaking analysis of the mission and thorough study of all details relating to selection, training and actual performance of undercover personnel.

Short Range Undercover is an undercover technique, which has the duration of short-range time. It may vary considerably, from a one-time interview to a series of separate, but related action over an extended period of time. It is a mission, to which short range undercover can be applied to include discreet collection of background information, preparation for a raid or search, installation or servicing of technical surveillance.

Undercover Operations are planned and executed as part of the overall Intelligence Project Plan. Undercover operatives can be given one or more of the following types:

- Multiple Assignments are a type of undercover assignment which refers to a single undercover investigator who is given the task of covering two or more of the above specific assignment simultaneously. This type of assignment can produce extensive information; with minimum expenditure of personnel, but the danger of compromise is far more prevalent. Multiple assignment are more commonly employed when the assumed role of investigator is a military role, thus making it possible for the subject and the investigator to be in activities without arousing undue suspicion.

- Dwelling assignment is a type of undercover assignment in which the investigator establishes residence in or near the dwelling which houses the subject in order to maintain contact with the home life of the subject.

- Personal Contact Assignment is special undercover assignment in which the undercover investigator is required to develop the friendship and trust of a target personality for the purpose of obtaining information and evidence.

- Social Contact Assignment is an undercover assignment which requires the investigator to frequent places of entertainment and amusement known to be habitually visited by target personalities and their associates.

- Work Contact Assignment is an assignment that places the investigator in a type of employment where he can observe activities of the subject at his place of work.

Undercover Operations are composed of three sections or units: the undercover operative or team; the Handler; and the Security Team. The Handler acts as the link between the undercover operatives and the Case Officer. The Handler plans meetings, is responsible for debriefs and any other assistance that the undercover operatives may require. The Security Team is responsible for over watch of any operational activity the team may perform, including contact meetings, and intelligence collection. The Security Team is also responsible for extraction if the operation is compromised.

Execution of the operation requires the Security Team to infiltrated into the Target Area first. After the Security Team is set up, the Undercover Team is infiltrated into the Target Area. The Handler ideally meets with the Undercover Team only in concealed, secure locations.

Undercover Teams report once a week, either through meetings or other secure communication channels. Long Term Undercover operatives must be debriefed every month with operational testing every two months.

Due to the risk involved, undercover operations are usually run only in areas under the agency's control. Operations planned for hostile or denied areas should be very detailed in E and E, as well as Infiltration and Exfiltration.

CHAPTER 2: UNDERCOVER OPERATIONAL PLANNING CONSIDERATIONS

UNDERCOVER OPERATIONS PLANNING CONSIDERATIONS:

Evasion Planning:

Escape and Evasion planning is included in Clandestine Operations because of the inherent risks involved in executing these operations. Undercover Operations in denied areas will pay considerable attention to Evasion Planning. E and E considerations should also be included in Area Assessments. E and E planning begins with a definition of terms:

- Evasion is the act or means of eluding capture.
- Survival is the act or process of surviving and remaining alive.
- Escape is to break loose from confinement or from enemy control.
- Recovery is the act, operation, or bringing one person, a group, or material out of an area of danger to safety.
- Search and Rescue is the employment of available personnel and facilities in rendering aid to persons and property in distress.
- Corridor is a specific route or distance within a contact area that the evader travels to establish contact.

- Survival, Evasion, Resistance, and Escape are the procedures, operations, and actions that may be applied by an individual or team isolated in hostile territory to return to friendly control.

- Hide Area is an area large enough to contain a primary and alternate hid site and is used for resting during the day.

- Hole up Area is an area used to obtain water, food, shelter, comfort, warmth items and to recover health.

1. Evasion is an act or means of eluding capture. Evasion can be classified as:

   a. Unassisted evasion-the evader or team receives no outside assistance and relies upon their resources to evade

   b. Assisted evasion-is evasion through the assistance of sympathetic individuals or other outside agencies such as established E and E nets to evade

   c. Short range evasion-takes place within the confines of an Operational Area and visualized as occurring in an area extending 150 km on either side of the A/O

   d. Long range evasion-takes place deeper inside the area bounded by the tactical battlefield area. Usually aircrews, POWs, and Special Operations forces will fall into this category

   e. Evasion by exfiltration-where the evader or team travels over land out of hostile controlled territory to friendly controlled territory

   f. Evasion by deception-is used when traveling through civilian populated areas. It may require disguises and cover stories. This category is often used in clandestine operations.

g. Combination Evasion-this is a combination of the above methods.

h. Evasion by deep penetration-is when the evader or team moves deeper into enemy controlled areas to elude capture or be recovered

2. Evasion/Escape kits should be stocked and cached in a secure but easily accessible location. E and E kits should be small in bulk, light in weight, and waterproof.

    a. Evasion Kit contents:

        i. Adequate amount of local currency or barter items to finance travel outside of threat zone.

        ii. Alternate identification documents if available.

        iii. Disguise items such as clothing, caps or hats, hair coloring kits or wigs

        iv. Contact protocols for support assets

        v. Phone numbers for local taxis, bus lines, transport companies, airlines

        vi. Key gun and hot wire kit

        vii. Backup/hide weapon(s)

    b. Escape Kit contents:

        i. First aid supplies

        ii. Water or water procurement supplies

            1. water purification pills or filters

        iii. Fire making gear

            1. should include five means of making fire

                a. lens

                b. matches

        c.   eight volt battery and four 0 steel wool

        d.   water tight container of calcium carbide

        e.   magnesium fire starter and steel

    iv. Food gathering gear

        1.   fishhooks and line

        2.   steel snares

    v. Shelter and tools to make shelters

        1.   knife

        2.   wire saw

        3.   duct tape

        4.   space blanket(s)

        5.   heavy knife or hand axe

    vi. Signaling gear

        1.   mirror

        2.   pen flares

        3.   whistles

3.   E and E plan format

    a.   Paragraph 1: Situation-addresses evaders physical condition, who/what he is evading with, terrain zones, climatic zones, vegetation, wildlife, civilian population, friendly forces, enemy forces, other countries if included in planning considerations

    b.   Paragraph 2: Mission-include type of evasion, beginning points and end points, and time considerations

    c.   Paragraph 3: Execution-

        i. Overall plan

        1. routes,

        2. points

        3. hides

        4. hole ups

        5. danger areas

        6. evasion is initiated by:

            a. evasion when not in enemy contact

            b. evasion when in enemy contact

        7. escape is initiated when:

    ii. Other missions

        1. escape

  d. Paragraph 4: Service and Support

    i. Survival aids

    ii. Evasion/survival kits

    iii. Special equipment

  e. Paragraph 5: Command and Control

    i. Chain of command in E and E operation

    ii. Recognition signals between Team and supporting assets at rendezvous sites

    iii. Recognition signals used at recovery sites

    iv. Signals should be verbal and non verbal

4. E and E planning considerations

  a. Initiate evasion when:

     i. Not in enemy contact-due to civil, military, political disruption or upheaval that prevents mission completion and normal exfiltration. Notification that mission is compromised.

     ii. In enemy contact-detection of enemy surveillance or impending raid

b. Hide sites will be determined from map study of evasion routes

     i. Hide site should have non military value

     ii. Away from all human habitation. Avoid built up areas, rural buildings, haystacks, farms.

     iii. Away from all water sources

     iv. Use terrain masking features

     v. Use densest vegetation

     vi. Plan routes to hide site

     vii. Plan escape routes from hide site

c. Movement to hide sites

     i. Plan primary and alternate route

     ii. Zig zag route or curly cue routes

     iii. Stay away from terrain of military value

     iv. Use terrain masking, all available vegetation for concealment, water sources for obtaining water

d. Actions around hide site

     i. Halt and observe

     ii. Listen

     iii. Link up hide escape route to area escape route

     iv. Check rendezvous points

           v.   Maintain security

e.   Actions at hide site

           i.   BLIS-blend, low, isolated, size

           ii.   Consider over head cover if necessary

           iii.   Do not break or cut covering vegetation

           iv.   Weather protection is prime concern

           v.   Maintain passive security while occupying site

           vi.   Avoid eating or preparing foods

           vii.   Do not occupy site for more than 24 hours

           viii.   Do not defend site

f.   Actions on moving out of hide

           i.   Sterilize site

           ii.   Move out to one of pre planned escape routes

g.   Location of hole up area (used for longer stay)

           i.   Must be large enough site to store items needed for next stage of evasion

           ii.   Hole up sites are located in even more inaccessible sites than hide sites

           iii.   Primary and secondary sites will be located through map studies

h.   Actions inside hole up site

           i.   Site is reconnoitered to confirm that site is isolated from human travel routes

           ii.   Escape routes are established

           iii.   Locate various sites in hole up site away from each other

        1. hide site

        2. watering site

        3. hunting or trapping site

        4. food preparation or preservation site

        5. tanning site

        6. meat drying site

        7. storage site

    iv. all sites should be located away from hide site

    v. foraging should be spread out throughout the site

    vi. "z" into site

5. Other Missions (sub section b, paragraph 3)

    a. Movement

    b. Actions

    c. Security breaks

    d. Training and rehearsals

    e. Movement by teams or individuals

6. Escape: Actions for escape

    a. Attempt escape at the initial point of capture

        i. Take advantage of initial confusion

        ii. You arc closer to pre planned evasion route

    b. Attempt escape during movement

        i. Take advantage of periods of reduced visibility

        ii. Take advantage of guards

        iii. Take advantage of transfer through civilian crowds, traffic problems

    c.   Escaping permanent facility is last ditch resort

        i.   Initiate escape attempt before physical deterioration sets in

        ii.   Careful planning is required to defeat enemy control measures

7.   Interrogation resistance

    a.   Cover with in cover

    b.   Stick to story

COUNTERINTELLIGENCE PLANNING CHECKLISTS:

1.   Names of Police, Intelligence and Counter intelligence units

2.   Names, locations, and descriptions of HQ and administration centers

3.   Locations of surveillance observation points and hangouts

4.   Locations of detention facilities.

5.   Names of individuals in leadership positions and personality traits.

6.   Description of unit:

7.   What is Modus Operandi?

    a.   Informant nets

        i.   How are they recruited

        ii.   How do the report

    b.   Surveillance techniques

    c.   Wiretap expertise

        i.   How or they used

        ii.   Who is targeted

        iii. Who approves wiretaps

        iv. Level of technology

   d.   Searches

        i.   How are they conducted

        ii.   Do searches need prior approval

   e.   What have they been successful at?

        i.   What types of operations are they good at?

        ii.   What methods were used?

8. Level of training and cooperation with foreign services?

   a.   Who trains them?

   b.   Level of training

   c.   What facilities are used.

OPPOSITION INTELLIGENCE SERVICES

1. Names of Foreign Intelligence Services and units.

2. Names, locations, and descriptions of HQ and administration centers

3. Locations of surveillance observation points and hangouts

4. Locations of detention facilities.

5. Names of individuals in leadership positions and personality traits.

6. Description of unit:

7. What is Modus Operandi?

    a.   Informant nets

           i.   How are they recruited

          ii.   How do the report

    b.   Surveillance techniques

    c.   Wiretap expertise

           i.   How or they used

          ii.   Who is targeted

        iii.   Who approves wiretaps

        iv.   Level of technology

    d.   Searches

           i.   How are they conducted

          ii.   Do searches need prior approval

    e.   What have they been successful at?

           i.   What types of operations are they good at?

          ii.   What methods were used?

8.   Level of training and cooperation with foreign services?

    a.   Who trains them?

    b.   Level of training

    c.   What facilities are used.

INSURGENT AND TERRORIST GROUPS

1.   What are the names or acronyms of Terrorist or Insurgent groups?

2.   What are their stated goals or objectives?

3.   What is the affiliation of these groups?

    a.   Countries

    b.   Internal and external terrorist groups?

    c.   Political parties?

    d.   Narco Terrorists?

4.   What personalities are associated with these groups?

5.   What are the descriptions and locations of:

    a.   Operational areas-rural, urban, combination?

    b.   Safe houses and support sites-Active? Contingency?

    c.   HQ-national, regional, local?

    d.   Training areas

    e.   Egress and ingress routes

    f.   Facilities available-ranges, hand-to-hand, classrooms, barracks

6.   Describe the equipment

    a.   What are the sources for terrorist or insurgent equipment?

    b.   What types of weapons are associated with the groups

        i.   Make

        ii.   Caliber

        iii.   Quantities

    c.   How are the weapons delivered and issued?

    d.   Explosives and incendiaries? How are they procured?

    e.   Vehicles?

        i.   Purchased or stolen

        ii.   How often do they trade out vehicles

      f.   Communications equipment

          i.   Where is equipment obtained?

          ii.   How are personnel trained?

          iii.   How well are they trained?

7.   What is their Modus Operandi?

      a.   What are their U.S. targets?

      b.   What are HN targets?

      c.   Other targets

          i.   Businesses

          ii.   Corporations

          iii.   Foreign country representatives

8.   What operations do they specialize in or have been credited for?

9.   How do these groups negotiate?

      a.   Face to face or by intermediary

      b.   Demands reasonable or not

      c.   Are there attempts to solicit media or public support?

10.   What are their intelligence methods?

      a.   Do they operate formal intelligence nets?

      b.   Is there evidence of infiltration of friendly or HN intelligence services?

POPULATION MOVEMENT AND CONTROL MEASURES

1.   What type of ID must be carried?

      a.   Photo ID?

      b.   Black and white or color?

2. What are curfew hours? How enforced?

3. What checkpoints or road blocks are emplaced?

    a. Who mans check points or road blocks

    b. What precipitates temporary checkpoints or roadblocks?

    c. What do security personnel check for?

4. What are prohibited or contraband items?

    a. What items are normally contraband?

    b. What are penalties for possession?

5. What travel restrictions are in place?

    a. What roads are restricted?

    b. What are the explanations for these restrictions?

6. What areas are off limits?

    a. What is the explanation for this designation?

ORGANIZED CRIMINAL GROUPS

1. What is the description of criminal activity?

    a. What is the normal level of crime?

    b. What is the level of violent crime?

    c. Is crime against foreigners more prevalent?

    d. What are high crime areas?

    e. Why do certain areas exhibit high crime levels?

    f. What is the normal police response to crime?

      g.   What activities cause increased police reaction?

      h.   Do police tend to over react?

2. What is the description of narcotics crime?

3. What is the official policy and attitude towards narcotics trafficking? International trafficking?

4. What is the local populace attitude towards narcotics?

5. What is the narcotics infrastructure

      a.   Type of drugs?

      b.   Organizations associated with procurement and distribution?

6. What are the locations of high drug trafficking and use?

7. What are the routes of entrance and distribution

8. What are means of transportation of drugs?

      a.   Air

      b.   Cars

      c.   Trucks

      d.   "mules"

9. What are the affiliations of traffickers with government agencies and personnel?

10. What are the affiliations of traffickers with terrorist groups or insurgents?

11. What are the affiliations of traffickers with foreign missions?

12. What are the affiliations of traffickers with other types of criminal organizations?

13. How are traffickers armed?

      a.   Type

      b.   Calibers

      c.   Quantities

d.   Sources

INFILTRATION AND EXFILTRATION PLANNING

1.   Infiltration is the clandestine entrance of personnel, documents, and/or equipment into a hostile area of operations.   Procedures used are designed to avoid contact with or detection by the enemy.

2.   There are four methods of infiltration; Black, White, and Gray.   The Black method in turn has four methods; infiltration by air, infiltration by land, infiltration by water, and stay-behind. This method seeks to avoid any contact with the enemy by entering illegally at any point on the border except a legal border crossing.   The White method of infiltration in which the infiltrator enters the country with legal documentation and has a legal reason to enter.   The Gray method of infiltration is entering through a legal border crossing with false documentation.

3.   In planning the Gray and White infiltration methods, consider the mission, personnel, the enemy, the situation, accompanying supplies, and equipment available.   The Black method considers all the above facts as well as; weather, geography, hydrographic, and distance.

4.   Initial Entry Report: Infiltration is not complete until IER is made to next higher echelon.   Format of IER in paragraphs is:

a.   Proword-this indicates what type of report is being submitted.

    b. Code Word-this identifies the Team making the report.

    c. Location-Give map coordinates and designated code worded location from which reporting.

    d. Casualties or Compromise-Report name and whether KIA, WIA, or MIA. Report compromise and initiate E and E.

    e. Contact-Report contact with local Assets.

    f. Additional Information-Report any additional comments or information.

5. Black Infiltration Planning Considerations:

    a. Air Infiltration

        i. Advantages

            1. Flexibility

            2. Speed and accuracy of delivery

            3. Short exposure to enemy counter measures

            4. Precise navigation

            5. Capability of delivering supplies greater than individual load

        ii. Disadvantages

            1. Vulnerability to enemy air defense systems

            2. Affected by weather conditions

            3. Possible injury to personnel and loss of equipment

            4. Requires specially trained aircrews

            5. Requires sterilization of infiltration site

    b. Land Infiltration

        i. Advantages

        1.   Minimum logistical support

        2.   Concurrent area familiarization and intelligence collection

        3.   Flexibility of movement and timing

        4.   Minimum interservice coordination

  ii. Disadvantages

        1.   Time Consuming

        2.   Increased vulnerability to enemy detection and interdiction

        3.   Limited capability for carrying supplies and equipment

c.   Water Infiltration

  i. Advantages

        1.   Long range delivery capability

        2.   Relatively unaffected by weather up until the point of embarkation

        3.   Operational briefings and rehearsals can be continued in route

        4.   Large quantities of supplies can be transported with surface craft

  ii. Disadvantages

        1.   Time consuming unloading and transshipment from offshore drop off points

        2.   Vulnerability to enemy shore defenses during landing operations

3. Possible loss of personnel and supplies during ship to shore movement

4. Limited cargo capacity of submarines

5. Special training is necessary

6. Additional packaging is required to waterproof equipment

7. High winds which affect surf conditions

d. Stay-Behind Infiltration

    i. Advantages

        1. Usually adequate time for establishing caches, safe houses, hide sites

        2. Support Agent Nets have adequate time to train and establish support

        3. Infiltration is simplified

    ii. Disadvantages

        1. Stay behind Networks are intensely targeted by enemy counter intelligence

        2. Team personnel must be thoroughly trained and familiar with Area of Operations

        3. Requires specific language training

        4. Special security considerations must be planned into communication plan with friendly forces

6. Gray Infiltration Planning Considerations:

    a. Advantages

        i.   Appropriate documentation can provide both cover for status and cover for action

        ii. Prevents tagging of Team personnel in future missions

   b. Disadvantages

        i.   Requires specific resources for documentation

        ii. False documents are prima fascia evidence of espionage

        iii. Requires specific training in appropriate cover

7. White Infiltration Planning Considerations:

   a. Advantages

        i.   Provides natural cover for status and some action

        ii. Itinerary can be designed to cover multiple intelligence targets

        iii. Use of cameras, video cameras, email, and text messaging are normal behavior for visitors

   b. Disadvantages

        i.   Suitable for short term operations only

        ii. Personnel can be tagged in future operations

        iii. Travel may be limited by diplomatic issues

        iv. Certain types of visitors are specifically targeted by enemy counterintelligence

8. The advantages, disadvantages, and considerations for planning an exfiltration are generally the same as for infiltration.

9. Planning considerations for Black, Gray, or White infiltration/Exfiltration methods will include at the minimum; a contact plan, plan for infiltration and contact sites, and plans for movement to a safe area.

Mission Planning:

1. Receive the Mission and Intent-Receive the OPORD and the Team Commander ensures that the perception of the Project Officer's intent is correct.

2. Determine Facts and Assumptions-Facts are statements of known data. Assumptions are used when facts are not available. Assumptions must be valid and necessary.

3. Conduct Mission Analysis:

   a. Review the OPORD

   b. Exchange information

   c. Develop a list of specific tasks

   d. Determine implied tasks

   e. Identify essential tasks

   f. Review all available assets

   g. Determine command and control

   h. Determine constraints and restrictions

   i. Propose level of risks

   j. Review facts and assumptions

   k. Prepare the restated mission

4. Issue Commanders Guidance-The Team commander approves the restated mission and provides his staff with initial guidance. Backwards planning is often used from this point onwards because time is often short.

5. Develop a Course of Action-COA development is driven by IPB, the mission, and the Estimate.

   a. Each COA must include What, When, Where, Why, and How.

    b.   The screening criteria for COA's are suitability, feasibility, accepta-bility, and distinguishability.

    c.   COA's can be graphics or short scheme of action paragraph.

6.   Analyze Courses of Action

    a.   The Team commander conducts a risk assessment for each COA to identify, assess, and justify risks. Risk reducing factors are identified and implemented or higher risk factors are accepted.

    b.   The COA's are wargamed against known or suspected Opposition Counter Intelligence and Security Doctrine. Record advantages and disadvantages of each course, continually assess feasibility, and avoid premature conclusions. Analyze each COA separately, avoid compar-ing COA's, and remain unbiased.

7.   Commanders Estimate-The Team Commander presents the best COA to the Project Officer for approval.

8.   Prepare OPORD-The body of the OPORD will be brief because the bulk of the Team's detailed planning will be in the annexes and appendixes.

    a.   Situation-1st paragraph describes the situation which prompts the mis-sion

        i.   General information, the background, a summary of the situa-tion and the security classification of the mission

        ii.   The Target and Target information

        iii.   Resources that will be utilized, including numbers and ranks of personnel

        iv.   Assumptions-any facts that contributed to plan as well as list of Targets or PIR to be answered

b. Mission-2nd paragraph details the objectives to be achieved

    i. Mission statement always begins with "To...."

c. Execution-3rd paragraph details how the objectives are achieved

    i. Concept of the Execution-giving a broad outline of how the operation will be carried out

    ii. Phases-Small operations will normally have only one phase. Phases are a way of defining breaks or transitions from on part of an operation to another.

    iii. Undercover Agent/Action Agent

    iv. Penetration method

    v. Cover

    vi. Accommodation

    vii. Cover Aids

    viii. Enhancement

    ix. Coordinating Instructions

        1. Handlers Training

        2. Screening and Selection of Undercover or Recruitment of Action Agents

        3. Undercover Agent Training/Agent Training

d. Administration and Logistics-4th paragraph details what support will utilized for the mission

    i. Case Officer

    ii. Handler

    iii. Budget

     e.   Command and Signal-5th paragraph describes the command structure and communications that will be used in the mission

         i.   Project Officer and Alternate Project Officer

         ii.   Case Officer and Alternate Case Officer

         iii.   Handler and Alternate Handler

     f.   Signature of Project Officer and signature of Case Officer

     g.   Distribution List-includes names of all unit members receiving copy of OPORD and copy number

     h.   Appendices and Appendix

         i.   Command Chart

         ii.   Security Instructions

         iii.   Statistics

         iv.   Target Folders

            1.   Primary Targets

            2.   Secondary Targets

         v.   Penetration Plan

         vi.   Budget

9.   Execute and Supervise-Each Team member completes a detailed plan of their area of responsibility.

     a.   Mission specific training and rehearsals are conducted under realistic conditions and equipment is checked.

     b.   The Brief back is given to the Project Officer and staff. The purpose of the Brief back is to inform the Project Officer of the plan with the approved course of action.

CHAPTER 3: UNDERCOVER COLLECTION METHODS

Surveillance

Surveillance is a planned observance of person's places or objects; however, it is concerned primarily with persons. Places and objects can be closely watched but are generally incidental to the primary interest of seeking information without people; the observation of human or physical targets by human or technical means in order to acquire information concerning identities, activities and contact of targets. Surveillance as employed by or against clandestine services personnel, may be stationary (observation from a fixed position) and mobile (foot and vehicular) or by means of surreptitious entry to make a search of the premises.

Environmental Survey:

The Environment is the setting in which the clandestine activity takes place. A through survey of the Topography, Opposition, Civil Services, the Public, and the Subject is undertaken to determine the methods necessary to carry out a planned clandestine activity.

Topography includes the broad, surrounding area, which must be entered into an intelligence plan. The number of lanes, the direction of the streets, traffic lights and heaviness of the traffic at a given time should be studied. Avenues of escape points of roadblocks and other physical obstacles of the terrain must be noted

Opposition: a term used Surveillance, which refers to the person, or group, which threatens the security of clandestine operations. In a given country these will include, in general one or more internal security and intelligence services plus a number of foreign intelligence and counterintelligence services. Each service can be expected to have some auxiliary support for agencies of its own government in that country, its own nationals resident in that country, or sympathetic nationals from other countries.

Civil Services is a term used in Surveillance which refers to a government services that include the civil police and fire departments, postal department, sanitation department and any other local government agency.

The Public is a term used in Surveillance which refers to local informers, stooges, and sympathizers of the local party in power, in addition to storekeepers, housewives and local public transportation personnel.

Subject of Surveillance - the person, place, or object being watched in surveillance activity.

Person: a term used in Surveillance, which refers to an individual; occupants and visitors of the building. The frequency and time of their visits are important. The number of persons staying in the building of various times of the day should be known.

Dress of Surveillant

The attire used in conducting surveillance dependent on the situation called for. (e.g. civilian attire for non-military subject of surveillance)

Close Surveillance is a continuous observation of the subject is maintained at all times, even if the subject appears to become suspicious or openly accost the Surveillant and accuses him of watching or following him.

Loose Surveillance

In Loose Surveillance, the observation of the subject is not continuous.

The surveillance may be discontinued if the subject becomes suspicious or when services of another Surveillant are required.

Fixed surveillance is a type of surveillance that is conducted when the person, object, or activity being watched is not expected to move from one area. The Surveillant may however, move from one vantage point to another in the immediate area. It is the subject who remains stationary. The Surveillant may move around for closer observation of the area and subject. When one Surveillant is detailed to watch a place with more than one exit, the Surveillant may have to move about considerably in order to maintain the proper surveillance.

Ground Surveillance is the systematic and continuous observation of selected areas, routes, or static location such as cross roads, bridges, or other specific types of installations. Ground surveillance is characterized by line-of-sight limitations, dependence upon terrain for movement and site locations, and limited capability for surface transport to displace surveillance in new areas.

Mobile Surveillance is type of surveillance, which is conducted when a person, object or activity being watched moves from one place to another. It's either foot or vehicle surveillance.

Moving Surveillance is conducted when the person, object or activity being watched moves from one place to another. In this situation, the Surveillant actually follows the object of interest.

Foot Surveillance is a type of mobile surveillance, which will not be detected unless action is taken by the subject to reveal its presence or unless the surveillants are accidentally or deliberately clumsy.

One-Man Surveillance: a technique of foot surveillance where one investigator is used to conduct the surveillance. It is best employed in a fixed surveillance. It should be avoided in moving surveillance because it provides least amount of flexibility in the surveillance. In addition to watching the subject, surveillants should take note, watch for convoys, and collect evidence. However, when the one-man technique of surveillance is employed in a moving surveillance there are some procedures that the surveillant should observe. When carefully and sensibly performed, the surveillant will keep the subject in sight for maximum period of time and with a minimum period of time and with a minimum danger of being made.

Two-Man or "AB" Surveillance: a technique in foot surveillance wherein the surveillant behind the subject is always known as the "A" surveillant. "A" follows the subject and "B" either follows on the same side of the street or form across the street. This move should be prearranged and signals should be necessary.

Three-Man or "ABC" Surveillance is the most effective technique of foot surveillance. It employs three surveillants, and is intended to keep two sides of the subject covered. "A" follows the subject "B" follows "A" and concentrates on keeping "A" in sight rather than the subject "B" also watches for convoys. The normal position for 'B' is behind "A". "C" normally operates across the street from slightly to rear of the subject. When the subject turns a corner, "A' continues on in the original direction of travel and signal instructions to the other surveillants from a vantage point "B" to follow subject, "B" now becomes "A" and "C" is then signaled to assume the "B" position behind "A" and "A" takes up a position across the street from the subject and becomes "C". When the subject turns a corner, both "A" and "B" continues in the original direction of travel and cross the street. "A" signal "C" to take up the "A" position. "B" then re-crosses the street and assumed his former "B" position. "A" assumes the "C" position.

Leapfrog Surveillance

In leapfrog surveillance, two or more surveillants are used to conduct this technique wherein this is a variation of the "AB" and "ABC" methods. It is simple to execute and greatly reduces the chances of the subject recognizing surveillant. Surveillant "B" follows "A". Both surveillants operate on the same side of the street as the subject. After a variable time or distance has elapsed by rearrangement or by signals, "A" falls back and allows "B" to assume the position "A" and "A" becomes "A". After another lapse of the time or distance, the surveillants resume their original positions. They continue until the surveillance is completed or discontinued.

Progressive Surveillance is a slow technique in surveillance, which is limited to subjects who follow habitual daily routines. The subject is followed at a certain distance and the surveillance is discontinued at a certain time and this is recorded. The next day surveillance picks up the subject at the time and place when the surveillance had been previously discontinued and he follows the subject for another short distance. This continues day after day until the surveillance is completed or discontinued.

Vehicular Surveillance: a type of mobile surveillance which may involve the use of one or more automobiles or other conveyances normal to the area, depending upon the sensitivity of the operation and the area in which the surveillance is to be conducted, as well as the number of vehicles and communications equipment available.

One Vehicular Technique is a technique in vehicle surveillance which is conducted by one vehicle following the subject alone and far enough behind to avoid ready detection. The distance between the subject's vehicle and the surveillance vehicle will depend upon the area of operation. In the city or building area, the distance should be close enough to avoid losing the subject.

Two Vehicular Technique is a technique of vehicle surveillance which is conducted by one vehicle following the subject at different distances on the same street while the other vehicle on a parallel street is moving in the same direction and receiving radio messages from surveillance vehicle which is behind the subject. This technique is more preferable than the One Vehicle Technique where subject's destination is apparent.

Four Vehicle Technique is a type of vehicle surveillance, which is conducted with four vehicles boxing in the subject. Radio contact is necessary among the vehicles. When in formation, the surveillance vehicle is in front of the subject. One Surveillant behind the subject, one to go to its left on a parallel street, and one to the right on a parallel street also. This technique offers maximum flexibility in that the surveillance vehicles are able to move with subject. In addition, if it is desired to make apprehension during the surveillance, it will facilitate by blocking the street on which he is traveling and closing in from the rear and the sides. This method provides means apprehension and lessens possibility of injury to by-standers. This method is only practiced in urban areas in which streets are parallel.

Reconnaissance

Reconnaissance is a mission undertaken to obtain information by visual observation or other detection methods, about activities and resources of the enemy or potential enemy, or to secure data concerning the meteorological, hydrographic characteristics of particular area. Reconnaissance missions provide specific coverage areas where there is a high probability or enemy activity and there is sufficient resource to maintain surveillance; an examination or observation of an area, territory, or airspace from the air either visually or with the aid of photography or electronic devices

Contact Reconnaissance: a search action to locate and contact isolated friendly forces, having communication failures, trapped in enemy territory or engaged in special operations.

Casing

Casing is a tool in clandestine operations, which refers to the circumspect inspection of a place to determine its suitability for a particular operational purpose. It is an indispensable preparatory step to the conduct of virtually every type of operation. It Is the visual inspection of areas or installations in order to determine their suitability for operational use, such as sites for safe houses, personal meetings, caching, and training of agents, communications or other operational activities.

Hearsay Casing: a method of Casing where bits of information are usually obtained from unwitting individuals regarding the target area. This should not be considered too reliable.

Map Reconnaissance in Casing: a method in Casing by using maps, which can produce a certain amount of usable information such as general and specific location and road network.

Personal Reconnaissance in Casing

Personal reconnaissance is a type of Casing which is the most effective but the most risky. The agent handler will have a first hand knowledge of the target area. He will be able to familiarize himself with the environment. Although, one should proceed smoothly and as much as possible not to arouse suspicion or attract attention.

Memory Training

Is a basic tradecraft tool which denotes the power by which we reproduce pass impressions; the power, act or process have remembering; or the total of what one remembers. Memory is like muscle. It must be exercise and developed in order to give proper service. One can be thought to have a trained memory just as one can he taught anything else. To remember, you must have the desire to remember, a system for remembering, apply your mind to what you want to remember, associates the subject with something you already know, and repeat it every now and then.

Observation

Observation is the use of one's sensory organs (augmented at times by technical devices) to recognize the clandestine potential or intelligence significance in one's physical and social surroundings. (The term "Description" frequently used in conjunction with the word "Observation" means simply the complete and accurate reporting of what has been observed). The individual's awareness of his surroundings, achieved through maximum employment of his senses. Expert observation enables a person to reorganize and later recall objects, persons, or situations correctly, fully and clearly.

The quality of any agent report can be no better than his ability to see or hear events of intelligence and operational importance. The sole purpose of observation, whether it can be casing, surveillance, watching a bridge being destroyed or examining an agent candidate is to obtain information. Observation is applicable to a system approach; selection detail; measuring dimensions; note taking; and memory aide.

Portrait Parle is a basic tradecraft tool, which refers to the given name to a system of identification of persons. It is a means of using descriptive terms in relation to the personal features of an individual, and it can be briefly described as a "spoken picture."

Long form or complete Parle is a type of Portrait Parle, which refers to the possible information about a person including general information, general characteristics and specific characteristics.

PHOTOGRAPHY

Photography for intelligence purposes are of the following types:

- Technical photographs

- Identification photographs
- Stop action photographs
- Documentation photographs
- Maximum and minimum depth field photographs
- Telephoto photographs
- Identification photographs at night
- Night target surveillance photographs
- Technical video
- Identification video
- Documentation video
- Telephoto video
- Identification video at night
- Night target surveillance video

In addition, field expedient methods should be familiar to intelligence officers. Alternate sources of photographic equipment should be located in case digital cameras are lost or damaged. This equipment may be obsolete 35mm equipment and the intelligence officer must be with operation of this type of camera and developing 35mm film. Officers should know:

- The use of binoculars as expedient telephoto lens
- How to load and unload film
- Identify and locate the chemicals and equipment to equip a darkroom
- How to apply the 5 step process to develop and print exposed film

- Expedient means of developing and printing exposed film
- How to apply the 5 step process to develop contact prints and enlargements
- How to construct and use an expedient contact printer and print enlarger
- How to construct and use an expedient film changing bag

The three uses of photography is; intelligence, documentation, and identification. For intelligence collection, many types of digital devices are used according to the situation, including cell phone cameras. For documentation and identification, digital cameras, especially with video capability are best.

The primary concern in Technical photos or videos is detail and clarity to identify unknown equipment, weapons and other artifacts. The subject should be photographed with a measuring device, either standard or metric. This measuring device should be standard to all Technical photos/videos.

The primary concern in Identification photography is focus to show the subjects head and facial features to insure positive identification. Posed Identification photos should include a height scale and name plate. Proper distance for posed photos is six feet. To take posed Identification photos at night, use a minimum of four flashlights to illuminate the subject. Optimum distance is closed to three feet.

The primary concern is shutter speed when taking stop action photos. Shutter speed of 1/125 is required for stop action. In low light conditions panning photography techniques are required.

The primary concern for documentation photography is maximum depth of field and sharp focus.

The primary concern for depth of field photography is lens aperture and f/stop. The smaller lens aperture the greater the depth of field (area of focus). The greater lens aperture, the less the depth of field.

The primary concern when using binoculars as an expedient telephoto lens is using the correct f/ setting and camera/binocular focusing combination.

The primary concern when taking target surveillance photos or videos at night is to obtain good images under existing light conditions. Many digital cameras have night vision and telephoto lens's that make them ideal for these conditions.

Elicitation

Elicitation is an indirect form of interrogation, which is characterized by the obtaining of information through subterfuge. It is a subtle form of indirect interrogation in which an apparently casual conversation is directed in such manner as to obtain information without the subject being aware of a deliberate attempt to gain significant information from him: the acquisition of desired information during conversation without the target personality becoming aware that he is being exploited for intelligence purposes or a process of direct inter-communication in which one or more of the parties to the communication are unaware of the specific purposes of the conversation.

Elicitation interviews are structured in sequential steps. These steps must always be included in the interview:

- Gain Rapport
- Engage in non-pertinent conversation
- The Approach
- Directed Questioning with Probes if necessary
- Disengage through non-pertinent conversation
- Terminate the Interview

ELICITATION TECHNIQUES:

Elicitation-an indirect form of interrogation, in which information is obtained by subterfuge. It is a subtle form of interrogation which uses casual conversation directed in such a manner so that the subject is unaware that information is being drawn from him.

Interview-gathering information through conversation with an individual who knows that he is giving wanted information but is unaware of the clandestine sponsor, connections, and purpose of the interviewer.

Probe- a term used in elicitation for a devise that serves to channel and direct the conversation. The use of the proper probe is usually indicated by the approach selected after a careful psychological analysis subject.

APPROACHES

JOE BLOW APPROACH-The elicitor adopts the position of an expert on all things. The more self important and obnoxious the elicitor is in this approach, the better it is. Subject is goaded into indiscretions to set the record straight.

TEACHER-PUPIL APPROACH-This is an approach that solicits the subject's opinion by insinuating that the subject is an expert in the field and you are eager to learn from him.

KINDRED SOUL APPROACH-This approach has two elements; you set the subject up on a pedestal for having some special skill or knowledge that you have long admired, and second; you flatter him by showing concern for his talent by giving him special attention. The danger is the subject may attempt his own elicitation.

MAN FROM MISSOURI APPROACH- The elicitor adopts an unbelieving pose about anything and everything the subject says. He questions all statements and propositions. Then, either alone or with the help of a confederate a sensitive subject is introduced. The subject may be induced to expound on the subject either through irritation or through the desire to explain the correct and accurate viewpoint. This approach can be often combined with the Teacher-Pupil approach.

NATIONAL PRIDE APPROACH- An elicitation designed to take advantage of a person's propensity to defend their country and its policies. This elicitation is useful particularly if the country presents the front that it is never wrong. This approach can also be used as a probe to goad the subject into talking about something they should not be discussing.

TEASER BAIT APPROACH- In this approach the elicitor accumulates sources of knowledge about a particular subject. He inserts into the conversation items that he knows to be true and gives the impression that he knows more than he is stating. The danger is that the subject may confirm the information that you stated just to give you the wrong impression.

PROVOCATIVE APPROACH- This is an approach which covers a wide range of conversational gambits. These gambits may range from the outright insulting to total boorishness the seemingly innocuous. This approach is designed to induce the subject to defend his position, state his creed, or correct a wrong impression.

ELICITATION DURING CONVERSATION

Probe is a term used in interrogation which refers to a device that channels and directs the conversation. The choice of the proper probe to use requires the same psychological insight into and appraisal of the source. The choice of the proper approach in many cases will also indicate the proper probe.

CLARITY PROBE is a probe used in case of unclear response. Typical way: "I agree with what you said, but I am unclear as to what you mean by…"

COMPLETION PROBE-is used when response is vague, ambiguous, incomplete, or too generalized. The subject is directed to expound and give more details on the subject without him knowing it. This Probe is often effective when used with the "teacher-pupil approach". Typical use: "what you said is too difficult to understand for me, a mere layman. Could you explain it so I could understand it better?"

HIGH PRESSURE PROBE-is a type of probe that is the natural companion to the Provocative Approach. It is used to pin down the subject on a particular point or to point out a contradiction in something the subject said. The High Pressure Probe is used as a last resort when it is apparent that nothing else will work. The biggest danger is that the subject may realize what is going on. The interrogator may end the conversation at that point.

HYPOTHETICAL PROBE-Is a probe that prescribes a hypothetical situation, one that is analogous to a real situation. The subject may express an opinion about the hypothetical situation, which does not exist, when they will not talk about the real situation. The hypothetical situation can be associated with a thought or an idea that has already been expressed by the subject with the hope that the subject will talk further.

NEGATIVE PROBE- is an approach that seeks to make the person react by saying, "No one could possibly know...", or by appearing bored, or disinterested in subject. This probe can be combined with the Blow Approach.

PARTIAL DISAGREEMENT PROBE- is an elicitation that seeks to get the subject to talk by saying, "I'm not sure I fully agree with you..."

INTERROGATION

INTERROGATION TECHNIQUES

Interrogation- is a basic tradecraft tool referring to a systematic effort to procure information by risk controlled questioning and influencing the attitude of a person who is uncooperative but remains in the control of the interrogator.

Interview-is gathering information through conversation with a person who knows that he is giving wanted information but is not aware of the clandestine sponsor, connections, and purposes of the interviewer.

Planning and Preparation Phase of Interrogation

Planning and Preparation Phase of Interrogation-Once the senior interrogator has assigned specific sources to his interrogators, the interrogators develop a plan for their interrogations. These plans reflect the current situation and the commanders PIR and IR. If they do not, the subsequent interrogation will not help the elements to satisfy its assigned collection mission, and the information needed by the supported unit will be missed. Each interrogator where feasible, begins his preparation by examining the situation map, the OB database, and pertinent information contained in the elements POW files. Here the interrogator gathers information on the sources circumstances of capture, comments with others who have been with the source, information on the source's observed behavior, and information on some of the sources personality traits and peculiarities from the screening sheet. This information helps the interrogator develop a picture of the source and enables him to select the approaches most likely to work.

An Approach is an intelligence process of getting people to talk, particularly during Elicitation, Interviews, and Interrogation.

Interrogation Approaches- These are techniques used by interrogators to gain the cooperation of the source to cause him to answer questions. One interrogator working alone may use approach techniques, however mostly two or more interrogators working as a team perform approach techniques. The tactical situation is normally very fluid and the commander needs information in the shortest possible time.

Approach Phase of Interrogation

Approach Phase of Interrogation-is an interrogation phase that comes into effect as soon as the interrogator comes into contact with the source and continues until the source begins answering questions pertinent to the objective of the interrogation. The interrogator does not run an approach according to a set pattern or routine. All approaches in interrogations have the following purposes in common: basic concept and approach techniques. Interrogation Approaches are techniques used by interrogators to gain the cooperation of the source to cause him to answer questions. One interrogator working alone may use approach techniques, however mostly two or more interrogators working as a team perform approach techniques. The tactical situation is normally very fluid and the commander needs information in the shortest possible time. Some of the most common approaches are:

- Direct Approach- An approach in Interrogation often called no approach at all, but it is the most effective of all approaches. It is the questioning of the source without using any approach at all. It is best used in sources that offer little or no resistance. It is used to create the maximum amount of cooperation in the minimum amount of time. It enables the questioner to quickly and completely exploit the information the source possesses.

- Emotional approach- a technique used during the Approach Phase of Interrogation, which consists of playing upon the emotions of the source in order to bring out the desired information. When using this approach the interrogator creates an atmosphere of emotional confusions designed to reduce security consciousness. The emotional approach utilizes love, hate, revenge, jealousy, pity and similar emotions. It also exploits religious and patriotic feelings, sense of social duty and other concepts based on emotional reactions.

- File and Dossier Approach- a technique in the Approach Phase of Interrogation, which is normally used in conjunction with the "We know all" approach. The interrogator prepares a dossier containing all available information obtained from records and documents concerning the source or his organization. Careful arrangement of the material within the file may give the illusion that it contains more information than what is actually there. The file may be padded with extra paper, properly indexed with the necessary titles. The interrogator confronts the source at the beginning of the interrogation and explains that intelligence has provided a complete record of every significant event in the sources life; therefore it would be useless to resist interrogation. The interrogator may read a few selected bits of the record to further impress the source.

- Futility Approach- a technique in the Approach Phase of Interrogation used to make believe that it is useless to resist interrogation. This is most effective when the Interrogator can play upon doubts that already exist in the source's minds. There are many variations of this approach. The interrogator may describe the source's frightening memories of death on the battlefield as an everyday occurrence for his forces. The interrogator must present factual or seemingly factual information in a factual, persuasive, logical manner and matter of fact voice. Making the situation hopeless allows the source to rationalize his actions, especially if that action is cooperating with the interrogator. The interrogator should be aware of, and able to exploit the source's moral, emotional, psychological, and sociological weaknesses. The futility approach must be orchestrated with other approaches.

- Good Samaritan Approach- is an approach technique used in the Approach Phase of Interrogation. It refers to the sincere and valid offer of help and assistance that is made to the source. You may first offer some innocuous service such as the loan of a car and work around to the loan of a book or periodical, the very title will indicate and point to a area of interest. The essential element is flattery, "I think enough of you to do things for you,-you are a fine fellow".

- Incentive Approach-is a technique used in the Approach Phase of Interrogation which basically rewards the source for his cooperation, but it must enforce positive behavior. Satisfying the source's needs does this. This can be effective only if the source is unaware of his rights and privileges.(POWs) Incentive must seem to be logical and possible. An interrogator must not promise anything that cannot be delivered. Instead of promising unequivocally that a source will receive a certain thing, such as political asylum or amnesty, the interrogator should promise to do what ever he can to help achieve the source's desired goal, as long as the source cooperates.

- Kindred Soul Approach-see Elicitation.

- Mutt and Jeff (Friend and Foe) Approach-is an approach in Interrogation which involves a psychological ploy. The source is being detained and questioned. Use of this technique requires the use of two experienced interrogators who are both convincing actors. Basically the two interrogators will display opposing personalities and attitudes towards the source. For example the first interrogator is very formal and displays an unsympathetic attitude towards the source. He must be very strict and order the source to follow what he says during the questioning. The goal of the technique is to make the source feel cut off from his comrades. When the source displays emotions of hopelessness and loneliness, the second interrogator appears. He scolds the first interrogator and then apologizes to the source, perhaps offers him some comforts. Then he explains that the actions of the first interrogator are the result of an inferior intellect and lack of human sensitivity. The source is then inclined to have feelings of gratitude towards the second interrogator, who continues to show sympathy for the source in an effort to increase the rapport and control the questioning which will follow.

Should the source's cooperation begin to fade, the second interrogator can hint that the first interrogator may return to continue his questioning. When used against the proper source, this method will normally gain the source's complete cooperation.

- Provocative Approach- is an Interrogation Approach that covers a wide range of conversational gambits. This may range from outright insulting, to downright boorishness, to seemingly innocuous. This approach is designed to induce the subject to defend his position, to state his creed, or to attempt to correct a wrong impression.

- "We Know All" Approach-is an interrogation technique which may be used along with the File and Dossier Approach or by itself. The interrogator must first become thoroughly familiar with the We Know All technique. The interrogator prepares a dossier containing all available information obtained from records and documents concerning the source or his organization. Careful arrangement of the documents within the dossier may give the impression of containing more data than is actually there. The file maybe padded with paper and indexed with all necessary titles. The interrogator confronts the source with the dossier at the beginning of the interrogation and explains to him that intelligence has provided a complete record of every significant happening in the sources life. The interrogator further impresses the source by explaining it would be useless to resist known data. The success of this technique depends on the naivety of the source, the volume of data on the subject, and the skill of the interrogator in convincing the source.

Questioning Phase of Interrogation

Questioning Phase of Interrogation-Although there is not fixed point in which the Approach Phase ends and the Questioning Phase begins, generally the questioning phase commences when the source begins to answer pertinent questions about the specific objectives of the interrogation. Questions should be comprehensive enough to ensure that the topic of interest is thoroughly explored. Answers should establish who, what, when, where, how, and if possible why. Questions should be presented in a logical sequence to be certain that no topic of interest is neglected. A series of questions following a chronological sequence is frequently employed, but this by no means the only logical method of answering questions. Adherence to a sequence should not deter the interrogator from exploring information leads as they are obtained. The Interrogator should master the following tactics to insure a productive interrogation:

- Prepared Questions are questions developed in advance of an interrogation to gain precise wording or the most desirable questioning sequence. They are used primarily in interrogations which are technical in nature, require legal precision, or cover a number of specific topics. Interrogators must not allow the use of prepared questions to restrict the scope and flexibility of their interrogations.

- Non Pertinent Questions-are a questioning technique in Interrogations which conceal the interrogators objectives or strengthen rapport with the source. They may also be used to break the source's concentration, particularly if the interrogator believes the source is lying. It is hard for the source to be a convincing liar if his concentration is frequently broken.

- Direct Questioning is a straightforward question in the Questioning Phase of Interrogation used by the interrogator due to critical time factors. It uses only properly formed, direct questions; properly uses follow up questions for complete information; properly uses repeated, controlled, prepared and non pertinent questions to control interrogation and assess source; avoid confusing, ambiguous, and time confusing questions; and uses proper logical sequence of topics or questions.

The interrogator should also frequently check the truthfulness of the subject. These checks should be done several times during the interrogation. Two tactics are utilized in truthfulness checks:

- Control questions are utilized in the Questioning phase of Interrogations, and are developed from information the questioner believes to be true. Control questions are based on information which has been recently confirmed or on information that is not likely to have changed. They are used to check the truthfulness of the sources' responses and should be mixed in with other questions throughout the interrogation.

- Repeated Questions are questions used by the interrogator to ask the source for the same information obtained in response to earlier questions. They may be exact repetitions of the previous question, or the previous question may be rephrased or other wise disguised. Repeated questions may be used to check the consistency of the source's previous response. They may also be used to check the accuracy of important details such as names, places, dates, and component parts of technical equipment.

Questioning techniques to be avoided:

- Compound Question is a type of question in the Questioning phase of interrogation that asks for at least two different types of information. They are in effect, two or more questions combined as one. They require the source to supply a separate answer to each part of the question. Compound questions should not be asked because they allow the source to evade part of the question or give an incomplete answer. They may confuse the source or cause the questioner to misunderstand the answer.

- Leading Questions are a type of question in the Questioning Phase of Interrogation which leads the source to answer with what he believes the interrogator wants to hear. As a result the response may be inaccurate or incomplete. Leading questions are usually avoided during interrogations; however the experienced interrogator may use them to verify the truth of a topic, particularly during map tracking.

Reporting Phase of Interrogation

Reporting Phase of Interrogation-is the phase where reports are submitted on all information of intelligence value that is obtained. Initial reports are submitted electronically whenever possible to insure that information reaches the intelligence analyst in the shortest possible time. Written reports are prepared in order to document electronic reports. Written reports are used as the initial means of reporting only when electronic reporting is not available. Any information of intelligence value that will diminish with the passage of time should be SALUTE reported. Electronic SALUTE reports are formatted and submitted according to the procedures established during the senior interrogators initial coordination. Information which will help satisfy the commanders requirements are included. Since these requirements will differ with each level of command, when conducting PIR or IR interrogations, non applicable paragraphs may be deleted.

Part II

AGENT OPERATIONS

CHAPTER 4

MISSION ANALYSIS

The Sponsor is the government (or other organization), which authorizes, controls, and supports clandestine activity. The clandestine organization, which carries out such activity, is considered an integral part of the "sponsor".

The Target is a a country, area, installation, agency, or person against which intelligence operations are directed; the person, place, thing, or action against which clandestine activity is directed.

A Threat Target is any group, organization, installation, or activity designated as threat to national security. Any foreign organization, group, activity or installation is designated as operational target. High risk foreign national can be designated as Threat Targets. The are categorized as Actively and Nominally Involved Personalities. Actively involved personalities are those that meet any two of the following indicators

- exert maximum degree of influence on the group or organization
  - o   ranking officer

o   involved in policy making

- engage in activities beyond the issues or concerns of their sector
- involved in fundraising activities of lcm
- involved in recruitment drives of organization
- participate in symposia, demonstrations, lectures designed to mobilize the audience to action

Nominally Involved Personalities: A person can be classified as nominally involved if he/she satisfies any one of the following indicators:

1. Active in open and legal mass activities but not in underground party activities.

2. Activities are only limited to the sector they belong or represent.

Requirements are descriptions, varying in detail and specification of information needed or results desired by a sponsor and assigned to a clandestine organization for action.

Mission Analysis begins when the Requirements are received. First determine if the requirement levied is appropriate to the unit's capabilities. Next, analyze the requirement itself. Restate the requirement and break it down to explicit and implied collection tasks. Study all past organizational experiences with target. Breakdown the requirement statement and restate it in the simplest form to aid comprehension. Then determine if the required information already exists in the units files. If not, determine if a Source is filed as having access to the required information. If the requirement cannot be satisfied with information on hand then a Target Analysis is performed.

Mission Analysis is intended to define the objectives, establish the operating limitations, and isolates the problems of the undercover operations by providing answers to some questions.

A. What are the specific objectives of the intelligence operation? What individuals, locations, or organizations are to be observed and reported on? In counter intelligence operations, what evidence can be collected?

B. What are the limits of the target area? Will the operation require advanced clearance from military or civilian agencies? Will the operation conflict with any jurisdictional agreements?

C. Where in the target area can a action agent be recruited to fulfil the levied requirements without compromise? Does the target area require military or civilian cover?

D. How much time is available for planning and conduct of operations before results are required?

E. Can the operation be supported logistically? What will the operation cost in contingency funds? What special equipment and materials are required?

Conclusion:

Mission analysis is designed to focus the planning effort to minimize conflicts and delays and answer basic questions about the planning process.

CHAPTER 5

OPERATONS PLANNING

Planning Steps in Operational Cycle

- As soon as the unit receives a specific requirement, a preliminary plan for answering this requirement must be formulated by the operations Section. The first step is that of operational analysis, in which the operations staff count its assets to determine what means the unit already possesses which would enable it to answer the requirements. Secondly, the staff makes the necessary plans to determine what additional means and sources must be exploited to fulfill the requirement levied. After this step, sometimes in conjunction with this step, all operational data, which has any connection at all with the target, is thoroughly studied. After this process has been completed, a preliminary operational plan is devised with the assistance of the lower echelon intelligence unit, which will guide it as to how to start the operation.

The Target Analysis determines the focus or target of the collection effort by identifying where the required information can be found. A detailed investigation of the target is conducted. The result of this analysis will be to isolate whether the Target is a person, place, or thing such as a document. Obtain all known information on the selected target and study all past experience your agency has had regarding the target. The analysis should yield the name, description, and location of the target at the least.

Target Analysis continues after one or more agents have been recruited as penetrates of the target, and incorporates the information provided by the agents. Good analysis will enable us to manage our agent operations more effectively and more securely, and will also provide a basis for crosschecking the information provided by our agents.

TARGET STUDY

A Target Study follows next to identify where and how contact can be made with the target and how best to collect the information. A detailed study is conducted to analyze means to exploit target vulnerabilities. Any secondary targets are identified at this time as well.

Each type of target requires a different type of study. An individual identified as a target can be analyzed by:

Where they live

Who they know

Where they work

Where they socialize or recreate

A complete investigation of the targeted individual will reveal patterns or behaviors that can be exploited.

An analysis of a State, Organization, or Corporate Target will include the following:

Organizational Charts

Methods of operation

Security practices

Requirements of supplies, products, and services

Population or workforce demographics

Manpower needs

Trade and distribution

Immigration or visitor policies

Official travel practices

Hosted events

A building or other location deemed a Target:

General location

Specific location

Type of building/business

Physical security

Shift schedules

A complete Target Study answers the following questions:

What are the specific objectives of the operation?

What individuals and locations are to be observed and reported on?

What evidence-physical, photographic-is to be collected?

What are the limits of the operational area?

What intelligence activities need clearance military commanders or investigative agencies?

Does the operation conflict with jurisdictional agreements?

What operational route can be exploited to penetrate the target?

Where in the operational area can an Action Agent be recruited to fulfill the requirements?

Does the operation lend itself to civilian or military cover?

How much time is available to plan and launch the mission before results are expected?

Can the operation be supported logistically?

What will the operation cost in contingency funds?

What special materials or equipment is required?

Order of Battle Intelligence is the study of the Target's organization, strengths, and capabilities. This process may be applied to hostile states, their militaries, paramilitaries, and law enforcement, as well as terrorist and insurgent organizations. Order of Battle consists of nine factors: Composition, Disposition, Strength, Training, Tactics, Logistics, Combat Effectiveness, Electronic Technical Data, and Miscellaneous. For collection purposes, a Target can be defined as:

Threat Target is any group, organization, installation, or activity designated as threat to national security

Foreign organization, group, activity or installation is designated as operational target

Actively Involved Personalities

actively involved personalities are those that meet any two of the following indicators

they exert maximum degree of influence on the group or organization

is a ranking officer

is involved in policy making

they engage in activities beyond the issues or concerns of their sector

involved in fundraising activities of lcm

involved in recruitment drives of organization

participate in symposia, demonstrations, lectures designed to mobilize the audience to action

The Target Study supports detailed operational planning

Target analysis continues after recruited agents have penetrated target

Incorporates information provided by penetration agents

Good analysis enables effective, secure agent operations

Provides basis for cross checking agent reports

Organization-This includes information on unit identification and organization. Insurgencies and terrorist organizations include military force, leadership core, civil organization, cadre and supporting force.

Disposition-Includes information on geographical location, tactical deployment, and significant movements. Insurgencies and terrorist OBI includes; operational, training, and supply bases, lines of communication, and areas of political control.

Strength-Includes information on personnel, weapons, and equipment. Insurgencies and terrorist organizations include combat forces, cadre, political support and popular support.

Training-Level of training is classified as: Individual, Unit, and Special. Insurgent and terrorist training is closely related to the tactics used and will include rigorous ideological training.

Tactics-Includes information on the enemy's accepted principles of organization and employment of forces for the conduct of operations. Insurgent and terrorist tactics include both enemy doctrine and conduct of operations in support of that doctrine.

Logistics-Enemy Courses of Action are closely tied to logistical support of that action. Terrorist organizations are less tied to logistical support than insurgencies when planning missions.

Combat Effectiveness-Includes information on: Experience, and Morale. Insurgencies and terrorist combat effectiveness can be described as the qualitative ability to achieve political and military objectives.

Electronic Technical Data-Includes information on communication and noncommunication systems. Insurgent and terrorist organizations often use less sophisticated off-the-shelf technical equipment in their operations, making analysis difficult.

Miscellaneous Data-Includes information on, personalities, unit history, uniforms, insignia, code words and numbers. The organizations stated goals and missions are also stated in this paragraph.

TARGET AREA STUDIES

A Target Area Study is a detailed study of all the available materials on the target area. This study will determine how the agent will be recruited, how communications and control will be maintained, and how the agent will be inserted and extracted from the operational area. Information is collected, collated, and evaluated on the operational area emphasizing the following:

Note documentation necessary for entrance into country.

Document entry procedures. Draw floor plan and sketch of facility. Document uniforms and weapons of customs and security details.

Determine Communication and transportation infrastructure, particularly public transportation in the area of operations.

Determine schedules, routes, and cost of public transportation systems.

Note television and radio programming, as well as newspapers.

Note local power sources; voltage, plugs, current, reliability.

Note telephone, telex, fax, internet, and postal or parcel delivery services. Note cost, locations, and restrictions of communications services.

Note exchange rates both official and black market rates.

Note ability to use credit cards, travelers checks, and foreign currency.

Note availability of expat jobs, especially with U.S. companies.

Living conditions and accommodations available.

Note availability, expertise, and cost of services such as mechanical, medical, food.

Note availability, expertise, and cost of professional services such as interpreters, secretarial, document and multimedia, and photo processing.

Note any no-go or restricted areas

Group or faction sentiment on current local issues.

Social customs, living habits and economic status of the area or neighborhood where the operation will be conducted.

Recent military or political events which might apply to the mission.

Note nationality and status (military, civilian) of non indigenous personnel, note area were spotted and activities.

Detailed updated road maps, aerial/satellite photos of the area.

Note names, locations, phone numbers, schedules, and personalities encountered of any facilities such as sporting goods and dive shops, golf courses, deep sea fishing, sailing, camping, shopping, red light, beaches, sports stadiums and gyms, museums and restaurants.

 Note names, locations, phone numbers, schedules, and personalities encountered at installations such as churches, libraries, theaters, embassies, public buildings, and monuments.

Note any ration control, population control measures encountered. Note procedures and documentation required.

Note details regarding the cost of both necessities and luxury items in the area of operations.

Other details that are deemed important as the planning progresses.

Target Area Studies are an essential support to the planning process. Target Area Assessment is the continuation of the Study after recruited agents have penetrated the target.

Target Area updates enables the safety of the recruited agent and the security of the operation. Information provided by recruited agents on the Target Area can be used to launch further agent operations against the same target to insure better coverage. This information will also be used to cross check agent reports.

A Penetration Evaluation concludes the Target Study. This evaluation focuses the planning on a specific vector to penetrate the target. A Penetration Evaluation will include at the least these points:

Will the operation be a Legal Operation or an Illegal Operation?

What method of infiltration will be used?

White-natural cover

Gray-clandestine

Black-covert

What method of extraction?

What method of penetration will be used?

Personal contact?

Social contact?

Vocational or professional contact?

Residential contact?

Technical surveillance?

Covert entry?

Target Penetration Analysis

Target Vulnerabilities-consider factors that illustrate Target Vulnerabilities, including:

Target Organization's Methods of Operation (MO)

Habits of Target personnel or of Target Individual

Target's Physical Security arraignments or organization

Target's geographical Location

Targeted Individual's Residence

Targeted Individual's employment and place of employment; Target Organization's manufacturing, supply, or administration facilities and personnel requirements

Targeted Individual's Social Contacts or Target Organization's Public Relations or Propaganda Unit's staff, organization, and MO

Penetration Analysis-consider all factors that could best be used as a method of target penetration, including:

Should the operation be a Legal or an Illegal Operation?

Can the Target best be penetrated through the use of Official Cover?

Can the Target best be penetrated through the use of Non Official Cover?

Personal Contact-Can the Targeted Individual be approached through personal contacts; Can the Target be penetrated and exploited by utilizing personal contacts?

Social Contact-Can the Targeted Individual be approached exploiting the Target's social circle of contacts? Can the Target Organization be penetrated through its PR, activist, or propaganda arms?

Vocational/Professional Contact-Can the Targeted Individual be approached by exploiting professional or vocational contacts? Can the Targeted Organization be penetrated by exploiting its interaction with professional in a particular area? Does the Targeted Organization require the services of any particular vocation?

Residential Contact-Can the Targeted Individual be approached by exploiting the Target's residence? Can the Targeted Organization be exploited by individuals who live in it's Area of Operations? Who live in the Target's anticipated Area of Operations?

Technical Collection-Can the Target be exploited by technical means? Consider resources available and the opposition's known countermeasures.

Control and Communication

What are the normal means of social communication in the Operational Area? How sophisticated is the opposition's technical surveillance systems?

What is the regular daily routine of the Operational Area? When do residents waken? When and how do they travel to work? When are deliveries made? Where are the markets, taverns/bars, government buildings, parks, schools and universities located? Do these facilities lend themselves to meeting sites?

What are the controls on travel outside the Operational Area? What are the controls on social and commercial communication outside the Operational Area?

What restrictions are in place to control foreign travel and foreign travelers?

THE COVER PLAN

Cover Planning is begun using information from the Target Study and the Target Area Study. Cover planning is a process that reviews each of the factors of the Target and Target Area Studies as well as the essential elements of cover. These elements are explained below.

Cover is a term used in a clandestine activity, which refers to the pretext or outward status, real or concocted, which is adopted by a person, organization, or installation to disguise clandestine tasks. It is a means by which an individual, group or organization conceals the true nature of its acts and/or existence from the observers. It is used so that the intelligence unit may operate with a minimum of interference from outside elements. Cover should be suitable, authenticated, backstop, mobile, financially supported, socially flexible, sufficient time and supported with intelligence communications.

Cover Story is a concept of Cover which refers to a biographical account, true or fictional, or a combination of truth, and fictional, which portrays the undercover investigator's ostensible past history and current status.

TWO FUNCTIONS OF COVER

Defensive Cover is a concept of cover, which serves to prevent detection of the operational activity or the compromise of operational personnel, and provides the sponsor with a basis for disassociation, or plausible denial.

EXAMPLE:

Cover for Status:
This is a concept of cover, general in nature and usually designed for relatively long term effects, adopted by an individual to explain his or her presence in a given area and his or

her general status in society. It is designed for public consumption and ideally should be sufficiently convincing to put to rest all doubts and suspicion by the opposition. Diplomatic cover, military cover, business cover and tourist cover are common examples of cover for status.

Organizational Cover is the type of cover used by a group of persons who have a constant overt association as means of facilitating their joint covert activities.

Group Cover is a type of organizational cover, which provides security for two or more individuals appearing to be working together.

Cover family is a type of organizational cover, which refers to the combination of cell and group cover.

Offensive cover is a type of cover, which provides access to the target and otherwise facilitates the achievement of clandestine objectives.

EXAMPLE:

Cover for Action is a concept of cover, which is designed to explain away or facilitate the performance of a given clandestine act. Although it may be an extension of cover for status and should be consistent with the cover, cover for action is not a substitute for cover for status; the clandestine operator needs both. It will vary from day to day, under certain circumstances, even hour-to-hour or minute to minute. For this reason, maintaining at all times a plausible cover for action is much more difficult than is the case with cover for status. When possible, cover for action should be planned in advance. When planned or improvised (as sometimes necessary), the two following techniques are useful in safeguarding the cover story and erasing suspicions of telling a lie.

Cover Conversation is a concept of cover which refers to a prearranged conversation that can be substituted for operational discussion should an unwitting third party interrupt or be in range of the conversation. Cover conversation permits backstopping should the participants be questioned separately about the substance of their meeting.

Concealment refers to a term in Cover, which refers to a technique or device used to protect a person, place, thing, or activity from unwanted observation. When there is lack of cover, or when it is inadvisable to put additional strain on available cover, concealment is an alternative.

Cell cover is a type of an organizational cover intended for small operating group wherein members of the group shows no connection.

TWO TYPES OF COVER

Natural Cover:

This is a concept of cover (for either status or action), which completely fits the true background and capabilities of the operator and is thereby authenticated and backstopped. Natural cover affords the maximum-security protection to any clandestine activity and, at the same time, allows for great operational flexibility. The person using natural cover is not likely to be unduly worried about the cover, is not apt to fear questions about the cover; and is in a good position to maintain the cover during the interrogation. If, for example, a salesman asked by a clandestine organization to go to a foreign country to execute a clandestine task, and he represents himself in that country as a salesman, his cover is not natural. Moreover, if he tries to make it appear that his overt employer sent him, this part of the cover story may not be natural. If a salesman who is selected is already assigned to the country in question, or who is about to be sent by his overt employer, a true natural cover situation results.

Natural cover story is a type of cover story which uses actual background data with minor judgment to fit situation.

Artificial Cover is a fictional Cover Story which is designed to explain the Agent's past and present activities. An artificial cover story requires both documentation and backstopping.

Backstop is a term used in Cover which refers to a falsified document and materials prepared by an undercover investigator to make his cover story credible.

Documentation of the cover includes documentation, which should be in the personal possession of the investigator or on file. Alias is a fictitious name of a person.

Aging the Cover is a term used in Cover as part of Human Intelligence (HUMINT), which refers to a situation where unnatural or artificial cover is being used. The individual's background is usually fictitious or false before the cover starts to operate. There are usually no facts to substantiate the cover story in the event it is checked. Everything will be real from the time the cover starts to operate. The individual using cover will meet people, find employment, establish a residence, etc. These are the real facts which could be checked and which could substantiate the cover story. Once cover has begun to operate, the process as "Aging the Cover" begins.

TWO CATAGORIES OF COVER:

Official Cover:

This is a concept of cover that represents him/her to be a member of the government office. He/she is ostensibly sponsored by an overt agency. He/she is permitted of free use of diplomatic establishments with their superior safekeeping facilities, security safeguards, and staff communications channels. The official cover is provided with access to official personnel of the target country. He/she is permitted to use official and diplomatic passports. On the other hand, non-official cover is usually less suspected and lends him-self/herself better to plausible denial by the sponsor in the event of compromise.

Non – Official Cover is a type of Cover in which the agent represents himself as purely civilian. He is free of any official connection.

DEGREES OF COVER:

Deep Cover is a type of cover according to its degree, designed to withstand close scrutiny by the opposition. A person under deep cover is protected by backstopping, which assures, at points where inquiry is likely to be made, that the cover story will be confirmed for example, if an agent claims to represent a   commercial firm, an inquiry at the head of office of the firm should confirm that the individual is in fact a bonafide member of the company, and all appropriate company records should carry information on this individual similar to that on any   other employee. As a general rule, backstopping the cover story will breakdown if the inquiry is carried far enough into the agent's background.   The important thing is to know how far the opposition can and will carry such an inquiry, and thus know what sort of investigation the deep cover can withstand. Cover authentication is a form of backstopping. The operator under artificial cover must take special pains to assure that all the appurtenances with which she/he surrounds himself or herself clearly reflect the cover story. For example, a man who claims to be an engineer representing "X" company would normally be expected to have a diploma from a school of engineering on the wall, membership cards to engineering societies in his wallet, correspondence with "X" company in his writing desk, and possibly tools and drawing instruments on a work table. These items serve to authenticate his cover. Needless to say, the individual should know something about engineering.

Light Cover is a type of cover according to its degree, which cannot withstand close scrutiny by the opposition.

Multiple Covers is a type of cover, which refers to the utilization of many, covers whether they are natural, unnatural or a combination of covers.

Cover Within Cover is a concept of Cover, which refers to a fallback story designed to provide a more suitable explanation if the first cover story proves inadequate because of artificiality, lack of proper authentication, or other reasons; the secondary cover in case of compromise, which facilitates the admission and confession of a lesser crime. A more suitable explanation if the first cover story proves inadequate because of lack of proper authentication or other reasons. This type of fall-back story is often practices by the subject of interrogation; the cover within cover states or implies that the person who was actually involved in a clandestine act was merely doing something improper or lesser illegality. The cover within a cover story does not admit the true (i.e. clandestine) nature of the act. For example, an illegal border crosser, if apprehended, might say when first questioned that she/he was hunting, fishing, or hiking, and wandered across the border. Upon closes questioning he might "breakdown" and admit that he was smuggling; this confession is still far less serious than an admission of spying, of which he was really guilty. Cover within cover is a common technique but it is often recognizable to the experienced interrogator.

Planning Cover for an operation is one of the most important tasks the Project Officer and Case Officer will perform. The Target Area Study is most important in this instance because the details revealed in the study will be used in the construction of a Cover for the operation as well the personnel involved.

Preliminary Plan

Use information from Target Area Study and Target Penetration Evaluation to formulate courses of action.

The requirement is analyzed to form a picture or profile of the individual who will most likely have access to the required information. Human social behavior and Organizational behavior is used to form a profile that describes the potential source's social, professional, and personal environment, his personality traits and his probable motivations for providing the required information. This Source Profile is used to determine the search parameters.

TYPES OF AGENT NETS:

Informants' Network

– a controlled group of persons who work through the direction of the Counterintelligence agent key informants or "cut outs," and supplies an agent directly or indirectly with intelligence information. It has three (3) types namely: Personnel or Individual Net; Key Informant Net; and Mixed Net.

Personal or Individual Net

– a type of informant network which is composed of an unlimited number of individual informants or "cut outs" controlled by and reporting directly to the CI agent. This type of net provides the greatest amount of control, but limits security of operation and coverage. This type of organization is also known as an Auxiliary Cell network.

Principal Agent Network is a type of informant network that comprises a main informant only and is not known to the sub-informants. Control over the sub-informants is exercised through the Principal Agent and not direct. However, the Case Officer and Agent Handler must know the identity, location, and other pertinent data about the sub-informants (provided by Principle Agent to the Agent Handler). There is more security in this type of net since the Agent Handler has been exposed to only one person, the Principal Agent. This network is also known as Intelligence Cell organization. The cell consists of no more than four members, the Cell Leader, also referred to as the Principal Agent, and three Action Agents. The Action Agents are not known to each other as agents and never meet as such. If the cell grows with additional recruits, a trusted member of the cell takes over as Principal Agent in most cases.

Mixed Networks are a type of Agent Network, which is composed of both individual net and a principal net. It is designed to give maximum coverage and yet maintain the necessary security. The two (2) mixed types of net (Individual and Principal) can be used on separate targets or individual informants maybe placed on the targets covered by the key informant net for purposes of supplementing and/or double-checking the information supplied by the key net.

CONTROL OF AGENT NETWORKS

There are three main methods of controlling agent networks:

Central Control is a method of agent control that requires approval for all actions from headquarters. This control method is the most secure form of control. Police intelligence operations, counterintelligence operations, and some counter insurgency intelligence operations use Central Control.

Internal Control means all operations are controlled from inside the target country. Operations are controlled by a Principal Agent.

External Control Operations in the Target country are controlled from a neighboring country. Control is exercised by a Resident Agent. This agent acts in the capacity of

Agent Handler or Case Officer. This control method is used when the operational area is under hostile control.

Dual Operations are operations controlled using both Internal and External Control to insure redundancy. This method is particularly useful when operating against very aggressive counterintelligence opposition. The Internal Control Operation should be tasked with the more obvious collection tasks, whereas the External Control Operation is a long term operation that emphasizes Operational Security.

FINANCING AGENT OPERATIONS

Intelligence Funds-are the funds for the purchase of information such as payment of informants, incentives, transportations, meals, billeting, representation expenses and other incidentals. Details and supporting papers are kept in the custody of the project officer until, such time the project be classified and ready for audit.

Intelligence MOE- is the budget for the maintenance and operation of discretionary expenses, which are technically known as the units' intelligence functions and activities. It includes funds for confidential/intelligence funds.

Funding intelligence operations in foreign countries requires stricter operational security than domestic collection operations. Use of the diplomatic pouch to transfer funds is often used. A support agent is required to open and maintain a bank account for receiving and disbursing the funds. The funds are then transferred to the intelligence team by a cut-out.   In some cases a foreign government will seek for reasons of deniability to finance our operations.   The arraignment is similar to the diplomatic pouch.   In cases where more deniability is desired, intelligence operations may be financed through an organizational cover or through criminal activities.

Conclusion:

Operational planning is a step by step process that begins with requirements and ends with a detailed plan to satisfy those requirements with manageable risk.

CHAPTER 6

SPOTTING POTENTIAL AGENTS

AGENT ACQUISITION:

Agent Acquisition

Agent Acquisition is a term used in clandestine activity which refers to the process by which potential agents are located, their suitability determined, and their eventual re-cruitment into the clandestine organization.

Spotting Step in Operational Cycle

The Spotting process is a consideration on how to obtain the necessary agent or agents who would be able to answer the requirement within the framework of the preliminary operational plan if our present assets are insufficient to if the type of target is brand new and no precedents are available. The first step in this procedure is to locate prospects for recruitment, keeping in mind the fact that they should, of course, have access to the information required, the ability to exploit the target, or any other qualifications, which would make their utilization appropriate. In order to accomplish this, we must survey focal points from which most of our recruiting is accomplished. By this, we mean points of interest, places where we can locate personnel with the proper background. At this point, it is important to note that the spotting program is continuous and involves all personnel assigned to intelligence activities. The fact that any given unit is adequately covering presently assigned targets does not mean that attempts at spotting new prospective agents should be neglected. The unit must always be prepared for any emergency of which the lack of agents is but one.

General Targeting in Spotting

This is a permanent requirement for all members of an intelligence unit to constantly be aware of recruiting opportunities that can satisfy requirements. General Targeting usually consists of a systematic survey of any informant population that may contain individuals with placement and access to the target. This survey is dictated by standard operational requirements and is focused on anticipated future needs.

The Case Officer should always keep abreast of intelligence reports and estimates to assist him in general spotting. Personal contacts, social networking, and special interest groups should also be thoroughly investigated to uncover potential agents. The Case Officer must be on the look out for any opportunity to acquire personnel rosters, membership lists, tax information, organizational charts, and directories of all kinds to mine for potential agents.

Specific Targeting in spotting usually begins with a new requirement being levied upon the field station or with a decision by station management to intensify or accelerate operational activity related to an old requirement. In either of these instances, the case officer assigned responsibility for penetrating the target will begin by making a thorough target analysis. Normally, a target is penetrated through recruitment of people who belong to it, work in it, or otherwise have access to it.

Target Analysis yields organizational charts, personnel rosters, directories, census information, tax information, utility bills, real estate information, vendors and suppliers, and organizations, unions, and political parties the target is associated with. Lists such as these are maps of points of contact with the target, points where it is possible to recruit an agent.

Spotting analysis uses information gleaned from both the Target Study and the Target Area Study to determine the potential agent's placement and access. Agent Placement is the position occupied by the action agent or informant in the target organization. Agent Access is the ability of the agent to obtain information relative to his/her assignment or position on target personalities/organization

A. Excellent Access- an Action Agent is considered to have excellent access to a particular area/field of a target organization or on target personalities if the reports/information he/she provided are evaluated or characterized to have focus/concentration and accuracy, regularity and continuity.

This type of agent has continuous access to the target and is able to do so without arousing suspicion.

B. Moderate Access- an Action Agent is considered to have moderate access to a particular target if the information provided by him/her is evaluated to have the following: concentration and accuracy, regularity and a lesser degree of continuity, accuracy, continuity and a lesser degree of regularity, accuracy, and a lesser degree of continuity and regularity than a Agent with excellent access.

This type of agent has access on a routine schedule, either regularly or irregularly, depending on the type of placement relative to the target organization/target personality.

C. Limited Access-an Action Agent is considered to have limited access on a particular field/area/target personality when he is not or can not be expected to concentrate his report on a particular area/field/target personality, with no continuity and no regularity.

This type of agent has access to the target organization/target personality but perhaps in a different division, department or unit. The agent may be part of an organization that is allied with the target.

D. Special Access-an Action Agent is considered to have special access if he/she is able to access the target organization or target personality with focus/concentration and accuracy once with no expectation of regularity or continuity.

E. Area Access-an Action Agent is considered to have area access if he/she is has access to the area of the target organization/target personality with no expectation of further access.

A Spotting Worksheet is useful to help focus the efforts of locating potential source populations during a target analysis.

Agent Spotting Work Sheet

1. Where is the Target active/or conduct operations? What states, organizations, groups, or individuals support the Target? What states, organizations, groups, or individuals oppose the Target?

2. What population groups have the Target affect positively or negatively? What population groups the Target interact with or support?

3. What Citizenship is population of potential sources with Access, Placement, and predisposition?

4. What Ethnicity, Tribe, or Clan?

5. In what City/Area does a population exist with Access, Placement, and predisposition?

6. What family names?

7. What occupation?

8. What Religion?

9. What Social/Political affiliations?

10. What Military service? Branch? Rank?

11. What Government position?

12. Which population/group/individuals is most cooperative?

BUILDING AN INTELLIGENCE ORGANIZATION:

When building a clandestine organization, each type of agent will be needed. The following is a work sheet designed to assist in locating required personnel.

- Agent categories
  - Principal agent/Resident agent
    - Directs activities of net
    - Controls agents
    - Performs administrative and operational functions
    - Evaluates personnel's performance
    - Operationally tests motivation, discipline, and security measures
    - Serves as screen Case Officer
    - Serves as intermediary between Case Officer and network
  - Penetration/resident agent
    - Individuals trained and tasked to carry out collection activities
  - Support personnel
    - Security personnel
      - Cutout
        - Delivers information and documents
        - Protects compartmentalization security of network
      - Investigative surveillance specialists
        - Watches and reports on activities of network members
      - Investigators
        - Investigates background of potential agents

- Technical personnel
  - Demolition specialists
  - Forgery specialists
  - Carpenters
  - Tailors
  - Technical surveillance/counter surveillance special-ists
- Service personnel
  - Spotting specialists
  - Contact/recruiting specialists
  - Training specialists
  - Safe house maintenance specialists
    - Usually a couple
  - Purchasing/procurement specialists

Asset Survey

This step is more important when planning operations in third world countries where lo-cal conditions and current events are not as available in Open Sources. Initial surveys are done internally, that is, within your own unit, agency, organization or country. External surveys are utilized in the event an asset is not available internally. Internal surveys are also utilized for locating potential undercover personnel. The Spotting Step in the Operational Cycle uses the Internal and External Survey checklist for General Spotting of potential agents.

Internal

Internal surveys are surveys of source groups that are under the Intelligence Agency's control.

Potential Asset groups:

- Individuals with expert knowledge of the Target or Target Area
- Individuals with external connections to the Target or Target Area
- Individuals who travel to the Target Area either professionally or for pleasure
- Individuals who host travelers from the Target Area for professional or private reasons

Internal Survey Checklist

1. Vertical Canvassing
    a. Is there a list of assets that are known and utilized as sources?
    b. Is there a department or division that specializes in the Area of Interest?
    c. Does any member of your agency associate professionally or privately with individuals or organizations from the Target or Target Area
2. Lateral Canvassing

a. What domestic military vendors are selling military hardware, software, vehicles, ammunition, or training and other services in the area?

b. What domestic airlines are flying into the area and how can the crews be contacted?

c. What domestic merchant shipping lines are shipping goods into the area? How can the crews or corporate officers be contacted?

d. What domestic companies are doing business in the Area and how can their managers be contacted? Who is running the Chamber of Commerce in the area and how can he be contacted?

e. Have domestic universities established Centers of Excellence regarding the Area?

    i. Archeologists?

    ii. Anthropologists?

    iii. Medical researchers?

f. What domestic religious or evangelical missions have gone to the area recently or are scheduled to depart soon?

g. What domestically based journalists are writing about the Target Area or have just returned from the area?

h. What domestic companies are running tours into the area?

    i. Individual climbers, hikers, explorers?

3. Retired

a. Is there a population of retired military personnel in the area?

b. Is there a retirement community or a population of expats in the Area? How can they be contacted?

4. Recruits

      a.   Are there applicants from the Area of Interest?

5. Immigrant/ Refugees/Displaced Populations

      a.   Is there an immigrant community from the Area of Interest?

      b.   Is there accessible refugee or displaced persons in camps located domestically?

Internal Survey Resources

1. Personnel Files
2. Alumni or Retired Association Records
3. Applications for employment
4. Applications for political asylum
5. Court records
6. Company websites
7. Government websites and official documents
8. Flight, and shipping schedules
9. Census records
10. News reports

External

External surveys are directed at potential agent groups that are not under the Intelligence Agency's control or influence.

Potential Asset groups:

- Disaffected, oppressed or displaced individuals associated with the Target
- Individuals, organizations, or groups connected to the Target or Target Area either professionally or personally
- Expert individuals, groups, or organizations unconnected with the Target or Target Area but interested and informed about the Target or Target Area

External Survey Checklist

1. What vendors supply laborers, food, medical, entertainment, travel/transportation services to the Target Area?

2. What manufacturers sell and have offices in Target Area?

3. What advocacy groups claim to represent victims of oppression, dissident ethnic, religious, or political groups in the Target Area?

4. What NGO's are working in Target Area?

5. What advocacy groups are promoting government, primary religion, dominant ethnic groups, or ruling political party of the Target Area?

6. What dissident or oppressed population groups exist in other countries?

7. Are there prominent individuals of the above groups that are accessible?

8. What journalists have written about the Target Area or travel to the Target Area frequently to write about it?

9. Are there resistant groups, competing political parties, competing criminal organizations, governments in exile, etc., that can be contacted?

10. Are identifiable individuals within the dominant political party, religion, ethnic or tribal leadership that can be approached?

11. Do you have agents with proper access and placement that can recommend a potential asset?

External Survey Resources

1. Host nation/ Friendly counter intelligence or security police files.
2. Common suppliers who provide necessary services and goods to Target Area.
3. Membership lists
    a. Union membership in occupations that supply goods, services to Target Area
    b. Political Party membership lists
    c. Business association membership lists of companies that do business in Target Area
    d. Lists of donors that give to advocacy groups either for, against, or victims of Target Area
    e. Special Interest group membership lists that encompass Target Area
        i. Recreational-hiking, sailing, climbing, caving, fishing, hunting, etc.
        ii. Hobbies-literary, art, etc.
        iii. Sports-tcams or individual competitors
        iv. Environmental groups
4. Local residents of Target Area
    a. Victims of oppression or violence
    b. Religious leaders

c.   Intellectuals-teachers, writers, etc.

d.   Business leaders

e.   Local tribal/government leaders

Asset Debriefing Guide

Debriefing follows a format that is designed to develop details that may be unavailable from other sources. Asset debriefing formats are designed for specific collection purposes. The following format differs considerably from a debriefing designed to develop target information. One thing that each debriefing guide contains is Basic Source Data for vetting the source, and Motivation Data for designing control and recruitment methodologies. The other sections have two purposes; 1-To fill in mission essential intelligence details, and 2-To assess the access and placement of the source by verifying the intelligence.

1.   Basic Source Data consists of the following information

a.   Full name

b.   Aliases

c.   Present address

d.   Date of Birth

e.   Place of Birth

f.   ID number or Drivers License number

g.   Physical description (with photo if possible)

i.   Race

       ii.   Gender

      iii. Height

      iv. Weight

      v.   Eye color

      vi. Hair color

      vii. Scars or marks

2. Motivation-this section consists of questions designed to discover the sources motivation for giving information

    a.   Political affiliation?

    b.   Ethnic or tribal affiliation?

    c.   Religious affiliation?

    d.   Member of resistance group?

    e.   Why did source volunteer information?

    f.   Is source willing to provide more/other information?

3. Political Structure/Factions-this section consists of questions that develop more detail of target area political structures

4. Civilian Population Factors-this section consists of questions that will discover elements in the population that can be approached for various types of assistance

5. Dissident Political, Ethnic, Religious, Resistance groups-this section consists of questions that will discover organized groups that may be approachable

6. Security/Paramilitary Forces-these questions will develop latest trends and details of Security/Paramilitary Force operations. These details are essential for planning E and E, Infiltration/Exfiltration, and Intelligence Collection

7. Infiltration/Exfiltration Considerations-this section consists of questions about geography and weather for Air, Land, or Water infiltration/exfiltration as well as

border crossing areas, ports of entry, and documentation details for White and
Gray Infiltration/Exfiltration planning.

Conclusion:

When building an organization, first locate and recruit specialists: Spotters and Con-
tact/Recruiters. Then locate and recruit Security Agents-Investigators and Surveillance
specialists.   Next begin to recruit Technical personnel. Use these personnel to spot, investigate, and recruit a Principle agent or Access Agent. When these steps in organization building have been completed, the Case Officer and Agent Handler is ready to search
for a Action Agent and begin collection operations.

CHAPTER 7

INVESTIGATION AND ASSESSMENT OF POTENTIAL AGENTS

Investigation in Agent Acquisition

Investigation is the process, in intelligence, which results in the collection of information on an agent candidate. In its narrowest sense, investigation is a security measure to determine whether one should proceed with the assessment and development of the candidate and whether the candidate meets the security requirements for an agent. In a broader sense investigation includes the assembly and/or substantiation of all reasonably available information on the candidate's background, association, and qualifications, for use in assessment, development, selection, and recruitment, and for eventual handling of the person as an agent. The first step while questioning potential informants is to fill out a Basic Source Data form. This can be done during questioning of casual or incidental informants or during the payment of reward for information.

The completion of the Basic Source Data form is the beginning of an exhaustive investigative process. A good checklist to follow is given as follows:

- Agent investigation

- o   Investigation done by:
  - ▪   Record searches
    - •   Done securely to conceal interest in subject
    - •   Own data bases first
    - •   Governmental, criminal, civil, and credit searches
    - •   Document searches
      - o   To research what subject has written
      - o   To discover any references to him or about him
      - o   Done through Lexus/Nexus, etc.
  - ▪   Pretext or undercover interviews
    - •   Of co workers
    - •   Friends
    - •   Neighbors
    - •   Governmental officials in contact with subject
  - ▪   Observation
  - ▪   Surveillance

- o   Background information
  - ▪   Background
  - ▪   Associations
  - ▪   Qualifications
- o   Security measure decision point:
  - ▪   Whether candidate meets criteria
  - ▪   Whether recruitment should proceed

Detecting Provocateurs, Fabricators, Probes, Paper Mills, and Swindlers

Provocateurs are individuals employed by hostile intelligence agencies to furnish false or misleading information to confuse, discredit, or waste the efforts of the opposing intelligence agency. Many times they are introduced through refugee streams and then volunteer their services as informants.

Fabricators and Swindlers are individuals who seek out intelligence agencies for profit motive. Such individuals are often connected with émigré splinter groups and act out of desire for financial assistance or political support. The information they furnish is a mixture of valid but outdated information, open source news, propaganda, and fabrications.

Probes are techniques used to channel and direct conversation. Individuals employing Probes may be concealing something from the intelligence agency employing them. They also, depending on the circumstances, may be attempting to elicit information from agent handlers. Probes can be indicators of Double Agents, Provocateurs, and Dual Agents.

AGENT ASSESSMENT

Agent Assessment is the step of the Operational Cycle where analysis of the motivation and qualifications of an agent candidate to determine his suitability for and susceptibility to recruitment is done.

Assessment is the collection of information on the needs, motivations, beliefs, character and personality of the agent candidate, and the analysis of all the information which has been obtained about his personal and professional qualifications in order to determine suitability as a potential agent, the likelihood that the individual can be induced to accept recruitment, and the type of recruitment approach most likely to succeed.

Motivation is the tool that the Recruiter will use to entice the potential agent to accept the recruitment approach. The Recruiter uses observation to determine the indicators of the candidate's motivation.

The desire for profit is indicated by:
- Does the candidate solicit to be paid?
- Does how will spend the money?

The candidate must be tested as to the extent he is motivated by money. Test him by:
- Offering money
- Offer scarce or valuable items

The recruiter must also determine if short term or long term payment is the best motivator for the candidate. The recruiter must also warn of the dangers of sudden displays of wealth.

Ideology as a motive is discovered by:

- Does the subject read political books?
- Does the subject participate in political discussions?
- Is the subject a member of political action groups or parties?
- Does the subject make frequent comments about political events?
- What are the subjects voiced attitudes towards social reform?
- What are the subject's reactions to current events?
- The subject's ideological motives can also be revealed by his manner of dressing.

To approach the ideological candidate, the recruiter could identify with the candidates ideals. The recruiter could also suggest that the candidate could realize goals by working with the recruiter's organization.

Patriotism as a motivator is revealed by:

- What the subject thinks about patriotic subjects
- The actions of the subject in response to patriotic events
- What are the subject's feelings or emotions in response to patriotic events or subjects?

The recruiter must be careful with a patriotic approach because the candidate will not accept an approach that is alien to his patriotic ideals. Once recruited however, the candidate will work diligently under dangerous conditions for specific patriotic goals.

Fear is a motivator under certain circumstances. This motivator is used when the subject is caught in a criminal act. Addicts are vulnerable to threats to prevent them from satisfying their addiction. In extreme circumstances, threats are made against individuals dear to the subject.

These individuals are passive aggressive and are reluctant to work or take risks, therefore the threat must be maintained. The Agent Handler must continually give compelling proof that the threat exists.

The desire for personal satisfaction is revealed by the subjects behavior. The subject will ask for a personal favor. The subject will ask for a title or a position of respect or power. Negatively test for this motivation by asking if he will perform the task for nothing. He will counter offer. This test is good for revealing desire for profit as well. Test and exhaust all other motivations before using this one to recruit.

Approach;
Promise the subject what he desires if it can be obtained. Find some equivalent if what he desires cannot be obtained.

Professional goals

This motivation is most often revealed if the subject has

- Background in investigations
- Background in intelligence
- Background in police work
- Background as a private investigator
- Other types of security/investigative work

Approach him by offering to allow the subject to continue this type of work at a more challenging level.

Desire for revenge is revealed by personal history or in conversation with the subject. Be alert for:

- Loss of business
- Loss of property
- Loss of professional privilege or license
- Victim of robbery
- Victim of rape
- Other personal injury or insult

These motives are easily revealed. However, these individuals are emotionally unstable and distort the truth.

Approach them by offering sympathy. Show a desire to help and offer them the opportunity to join an organization or movement that allows them to work out their anger in a positive manner.

Conclusion:

The investigation phase is essential to prevent the compromise of the impending operation. There are three main tools used in investigating potential agents:

- Polygraphs
- Background searches
- Physical and technical surveillance

Short term undercover operations are often executed for the purpose of qualifying or disqualifying a candidate for recruitment.

Assessment requires a careful examination of the candidate's motivation and other qualifications to ensure a successful recruitment. The recruiter determines from the assessment analysis the primary and secondary approaches that will be most successful. These approaches can be memorized by the acronym; M.I.C.E. That is, Money, Ideology, Compromise, and Emotion.

CHAPTER 8

DEVELOPMENT AND RECRUITMENT

Development Step in Agent Acquisition

Development is the relatively long term cultivation of a relationship between a member of the clandestine organization and potential agent with a view towards investigation, assessment, and eventual recruitment of the candidate. This step in the operational cycle consists of actions taken by the recruiting officer to influence the agent candidate, to create a situation, which is more conducive to a successful recruitment, and simultaneously to reduce the possible damage should the recruitment attempt fail.

Recruitment Step in Agent Acquisition

This is the act of inducing an agent candidate to enter into a clandestine relationship on behalf of a sponsor and to accept some degree of direction and control by the clandestine organization; the process of persuading the agent candidate to accept a clandestine relationship and provide the information or service we are seeking. The Recruiter's aim is to enlist the services of a certain person in an intelligence operation. The more thorough the investigation of the prospect has been, the more accurately a prediction of the success or failure of a future-recruiting attempt. It is by analysis of the information obtained through investigation phase that the recruiting approach may be made. An interview is arranged between the prospect and recruiter and depending on the analysis; an approach considered having the greatest potential for success is chosen. In some cases, the direct approach may be sufficient, that is the recruiter may put his cards on the table and say, "I am a representative of intelligence. I would like you to work for me. Will you work for me?" In most cases, however, the indirect approach is necessary. The prospect must be guided by the recruiter towards a way of thinking which would make him vulnerable to the actual recruiting "hook". In order to do this, the recruiter must establish the needs and the motives of the prospect. The recruiter must convince him that cooperation with the intelligence activity would fulfill this need and must actually arouse a sincere desire within the prospect to work for you. Of course, all recruitment attempts will not be successful, even if handled in the most efficient manner. However, by adhering to the guidelines we have outlined, the optimum percentage of success would be assured. After an agent or agents has been recruited to answer the question/requirements, the final operational plan is devised. The reason why this could not be done earlier is that circumstances, mixed with some degree of good fortune, may have helped us on recruiting an agent who has much greater access than we have expected during our preliminary operational planning. On the other hand, it may possible that we were unsuccessful in recruiting the type of individual we planned for and would have to attack the requirement from another area.

Conclusion:

During the Development Phase, the potential agent is observed to continue assessment and to plan the contact with the recruiter. After recruitment the operational plan is finalized and a Case Officer is assigned. The Case Operation Plan is then submitted to the Project Officer for approval. This intelligence management policy reinforces the old adage "The man is recruited for the job".

CHAPTER 9

AGENT TRAINING

Agent Handling

This is a step in Agent Acquisition, which refers to the supervision and management of the agent and his activities so as to minimize potentially dangerous effects of personal and professional problems and enhance the likelihood of success in the clandestine undertaking.

Training Step in Operational Cycle

After the prospect has been recruited, he must be given as thorough an amount of training as time permits. Generally speaking, this training will be divided into four categories namely: General Training - This is to instill in the agent the basic concept of intelligence activities; Cover Training - During the period he is trained in concealing his true identity, his real background will be of great assistance in constructing a plausible cover or false story about himself; Security Training - The phase concerns both with the personal security of the agent and the security of the operations as a whole; Mission Techniques - during this phase, the agent receives general training on the "mechanical" procedures which may be of great importance during any mission on which he may be sent in the future. This would include, communications; the means of entering and leaving an area; the basic items of information about a specific area; the knowledge of which is imperative for any resident area; methods through which he may detect and evade surveillance; any other information which may be of importance during future missions.

A training plan checklist is given as an example:

General Training

Intelligence Collection:

- Elicitation training
- Intelligence photography
- Observation
- Casing and reconnaissance training

Communications-Three channel communications system

- Normal
- Alternate
- Emergency

Personal meetings

- Signals
- Cover
- Safe sites and safe houses

Drops

- Signals

- cover

- safe sites

Cut outs/mail drops

- Cover

- Brush drops

Codes and ciphers

Cover training

Used to conceal true identity

Concealment

- Technique or device to protect from unwanted observation

- Used when cover is weak

- Or when no cover exists

Cover story/biographical account are arrived at after analyzing the mission, the agent's personal history, and his personality.

- Parts of the agent's personal history that are useful for identification are kept and the rest is discarded.

- Is target area urban or rural?

- What travel restrictions are in target area?

- What types of travel or activities arouse suspicion

- How will he explain where he has been?

- How will he explain what he presently does?
- Cover should answer questions that security forces ask.To do this cover story should be:
  - Suitable
  - Authenticated
  - Backstopped
  - Mobile
  - Financially supported
  - Socially flexible
  - Sufficient time
  - intelligence communications supported

Natural cover

- Fits true background and capabilities of operator
  - Maximum security
  - Great flexibility
  - Used for status or action covers
  - Necessary to conceal relationship to intelligence agency
  - necessary to conceal reason for contact or penetration of target
  - Details will remain verifiable by security forces through each phase of operation

Artificial Cover

- biographical data is fictional-Details of cover depend on:
  - Mission
    - Cover should explain the agents status and action through each phase of the operation
    - Target area analysis reveals cover indicators that will insure protection through each operational phase
      - Agent training
      - Agent dispatch
      - Penetration or contact
        - Work
        - Personal contact
        - Social
        - Dwelling
      - Communication
      - Agent reception

Agent type

- Each type requires different covers that must explain Who, What, Where, and Why of agents actions
  - Principle agent or supervisor
    - Necessary to account for travel and many social and profes-sional contacts
  - Action agent

- Plausible reason to penetrate target
  - Demographic most likely to be recruited by target
  - Defector with valuable information
  - Political sympathies
  - Clan or familial affiliation
- Support agent
  - If non permanent assignment then usually short term cover
  - If permanent assignment then long term cover
- Service agent
  - Usually short term cover to explain actions

TYPES OF COVER

Cover for status

- Is what the agent lives every day

Official cover

- Represents oneself as government official
- Has use of diplomatic safeguards
- Diplomatic facilities
- Diplomatic communications
- Uses official diplomatic passports
- Has access to officials of target country

- Examples
  - ○ Military cover
  - ○ Diplomatic cover

Non official cover

- Civilian
- No official connection
- Examples
  - ○ Tourist cover
  - ○ Business cover

Cover for status

- Explains presence in area
- Social status

Cover for action

- Explains clandestine action
- Should be planned in advance
- Offensively cover
  - ○ Provides access to target
  - ○ Facilitates achievement of clandestine objectives
- Defensively cover
  - ○ Protects clandestine operations

o   Provides sponsor with plausible denial

Cover conversation

Individual Cover

Light cover

- Cannot withstand close scrutiny

Deep cover

- Fully backstopped
- Requires extensive authentication
- Aging the cover

Multiple covers

- Utilization of many covers
- Can be natural, unnatural, or combination

Cover within cover

- Provides suitable explanation if cover story fails because:
    o   Artificiality
    o   Lack of authentication
    o   Is admission or confession of lesser crime
    o   Explains clandestine action
        - Should be planned in advance

Organizational Covers

Group cover

- Two or more individuals
- Working together

Organizational cover

- Used by group of persons who must have constant overt association to facilitate joint covert activities
- Considered an artificial cover
- Used to conceal the identity of the agents and their activities as well as conceal the true nature and purpose of the facilities
- Type of organizational cover used depends on the security requirements and the requirements of the agents to gather information
- "Front Organization" is a special type of organizational cover where only a few of the "employees" know the true purpose of the business

Cell cover

- Small operating group
- Member identities known only to Cell Leader
- Members show no connection
- Used when cell members are of different social or economic classes
- Difficult to use cell cover in rural environment
- Most suited to urban environment
- Meetings are infrequent

- Uses holidays, festivals, sporting events, book clubs, educational classes, etc. as cover for meetings

Cover family

- Combination of group and cell cover
- Suitable for rural environments
- Allows for "introduced agent"

Security training

Begins immediately upon recruitment

- Agent should not make changes in spending habits.
- Agent should not change personal habits and patterns of activity. This arouses suspicion of family, friends, and associates

Personal security

- Taught to recognize and resist elicitation attempts
- Recognition of agents provocateurs
- Taught to detect and elude surveillance
- Taught to resist direct interrogation
- Surveillance and counter surveillance techniques
- Places and areas to be avoided
    - Areas and places controlled by security forces

- o Areas and places under surveillance by security forces
- Individuals to avoid
    - o Known criminals
    - o Politicians or public figures under surveillance by security or police
    - o Individuals known or suspected to be under surveillance
    - o Any individual under surveillance
    - o Any individual that draws official attention
- Personal conduct
    - o Entertaining too much and spending too much money
    - o Possession of foreign or luxury items that neighbors can't afford
    - o Frequenting locations that are raided by police
    - o Frequenting gambling institutions
    - o Avoid legal suites
    - o Avoid any controversial or newsworthy activity
- Security discipline
    - o Compartmentalization
    - o Agent knows only what he needs to know about:
        - ▪ Personnel
        - ▪ Structure
        - ▪ Activities of the organization

Specialized Mission Training

This phase of training can include:

Specialized communications equipment

Special disguise techniques

Advanced surveillance and tracking devices

Technical surveillance equipment and techniques

Conclusion:

Agent handling or management begins with Agent Training. The training should be comprehensive enough to allow the agent to perform the tasks assigned to him and designed to ensure operational security requirements.

CHAPTER 10

AGENT BRIEFING

Briefing an Agent

This is a phase in Agent Acquisition/Operational Cycle, which refers to the preparation of a person for a specific mission by describing the objective, the requirements, the situation he is expected to encounter, and the methods, he is to employ getting to the target considering the amount of time to be spent on target and the exact information desired.

Investigation Phase of Operational Cycle

After the briefing has been concluded, the briefer must interrogate the agent to be certain in his own mind that he (agent) has understood all of the elements discussed during the briefing. After this review has been concluded, meeting instructions must be given to the agent. The entire briefing must be recorded exactly. At this time, we should point out that the agent should receive all the training and briefing necessary for the successful completion of future missions to which he may be assigned. The trainer and briefer should make certain the necessity for his efficient functioning. The need to know principle applies to everyone.

Conclusion:

This phase insures that the Agent is updated on current information in the area in which he his expected to operate. The Agent Handler also makes a last minute appraisal of the Agent's preparedness to perform the mission. The Agent should be familiar with his documentation as well any equipment he is to use to complete the operational requirements.

CHAPTER 11

DISPATCH AND RECEPTION

Dispatch Step in Operational Cycle

The agent in this step is actually sent to get the information. This may be accomplished on foot, by air or by sea, depending on where the target is, time factor and other operational considerations. The infiltration may be either by the black method - that is by crossing a border illegally at a point other than a legal crossing point; the gray method - in which the agent crosses at a legal border point utilizing false documentation; or the white method - which more or less restricts itself to legal travelers who cross into the denied area with their own documentation through legal crossing points and have the legal right to enter the denied area. During this phase, it is important for the agent to have a thorough knowledge of the target, the target area and the third country when appropriate. This is especially true for agents using the black and gray method of infiltration. All of this, information equally pertains to the reception phase which is the phase when the agent exfiltrates from the denied area after completion of the mission.

Reception Step in Operational Cycle

-in which the agent Exfiltrates from the denied are after completion of the mission. The agent utilizes the White, Black, or Gray method to cross from enemy controlled territory to friendly territory to usually to rendezvous with Agent Handler or other contact.

Rendezvous Point is a pre-arranged meeting at a given time and place, from which to begin an action or phase of operation, or to which to return after an operation. The Agent Handler is responsible for issuing the order for the agent to shut down clandestine activity and proceed to the rendezvous point.

Conclusion:

The Dispatch step is one of the most sensitive in the operational cycle. During the infiltration into the operational area the Agent is exposed as he ever will be to detection by opposition counterintelligence forces. The Agent Handler can go far to ensure the success of the mission by consciously working to prepare the Agent in this phase of the operation. Reception:

The decision to terminate the operation and exfiltrate the agent can result from several factors:

- The intelligence requirements have been satisfied and continued operations may compromise the intelligence agency.

- The collection operation has been compromised and the operation is terminated to prevent further security breaches.
- The agent's performance is deemed unsatisfactory and exfiltration is necessary to prevent a compromise of operational security.

In any case, the exfiltration and extraction phase of the operational cycle is a vulnerable step and requires utmost attention to security.

CHAPTER 12

AGENT TESTING

Operational Testing Step in Operational Cycle

It is necessary for us to understand that the operational testing of an agent is a continuous process from the time he is hired up until the time that his employment is terminated. The fact that he has been employed in an intelligence unit for a long period of time and has been handled by other intelligence personnel (chiefs), with great success, even if the information he submitted has been evaluated very highly, does not mean that he is to be trusted implicitly. With no regard for his previous record, the agent must continue to undergo operational testing during his entire period of employment. This may include interview or interrogations between him and his chief to determine any change in motivation or qualifications. He may be given a non-existent target to cover, or he may be assigned to a mission about which we have complete knowledge, in order to determine his honesty in reporting. He may be assigned to a mission to whom another agent has been previously assigned, in order to determine whether he is prone to fabricate. In some instances, the chief may have him surveillance in order to find out who his contacts are. In other cases the polygraph (lie detector) may be administered. At all times, however, the chief must scrutinize the information and operational reports in order to find any flaws.

In this matter also, the intelligence staff will be of great assistance to the field in analyzing reports submitted by the agent and comparing them to other information not available to the chief.

Surveillance and Counter Surveillance

An important component of the Operational Testing Step is surveillance of Agent Net personnel. Surveillance is conducted to confirm if agents are carrying out assigned tasks to detect paper milling and the servicing of drops to assess professionalism. Support personnel are monitored to detect traitorous conduct and safe houses are observed to detect enemy counter intelligence activity.

Polygraphs

Agents should be polygraphed on frequent basis to discourage traitorous conduct. Any long term agent suspected of treasonable activities should be subjected to polygraph examinations as soon as possible. If polygraph equipment is not available, the agent should be subjected to integrity tests. Examples of integrity tests are: Overpay the agent for expenses to see if he reports the discrepancy, have another agent posing as a member of another intelligence agency approach the subject in a recruiting attempt to see if he reports the attempt.

Evaluation

Evaluation is an operation being done during the processing of information (Intel cycle) which includes determining the pertinence of the information, the reliability of the source and agency, and accuracy of information.

Information Evaluation

A - Completely Reliable 1 - Confirmed by Other Sources

B - Usually Reliable 2 - Probably True

C - Fairly Reliable 3 - Possibly True

D - Not Usually Reliable 4 - Doubtfully True

E - Unreliable 5 - Improbable

F - Reliability cannot 6 - Truth cannot be judged

Be judged

Conclusion:

Agent testing continues throughout the Operational Cycle. This serves as a form of quality assurance. The agent and information evaluation process is an important factor in the monthly and quarterly evaluations which determine whither the operation should continue or be terminated.

CHAPTER 13

Communication and Control

Intelligence Communications Step in Operational Cycle

 As soon as the agent leaves the physical presence of his chief after he has been assigned a mission, control becomes increasingly difficult. Operationally, complete control of an agent is impossible. To exercise partial control, a system of communication may be utilized. In order to make certain that the agent actually has physically entered the target area; the chief may require him to send a letter to him, which has been stamped within the target area. If it does not encompass any danger to the agent, the chief may require him to save receipts from hotels, restaurants, within the target area. Control to Agent is a term used in Agent Acquisition referring to any forms of influence used to induce an agent to accept more readily the direction and discipline of the clandestine organization.

The question of control of agents is just one of the requirements of Intel communications. The major requirements of course, are to permit the successful operation of this specific mission.

Communications are generally categorized into two parts - technical and non-technical. Under technical communication, we have photography, radio and secret writing. Non-technical communication includes couriers, accommodation addresses, signal, drops and personal meeting. Non-technical communication is used especially when the Opposition's counterintelligence forces have an unknown or well known advantage over your organization. The principle of Compartmentation in intelligence communication is of paramount importance. It must be constructed in such a manner that the compromise of one part of the operation would not eliminate the operation as a whole but would establish, a "dead end" for any opposition intelligence investigations. To ensure continuity of communication, a redundant system must be planned. There should be a Primary, an Alternate, and a Emergency communication channel. The Primary channel should be the most secure, the Alternate channel has the same level of security and is used incase the Primary is unavailable. The Emergency channel should be the quickest and most direct. Security is not as important an issue here because the operation is already compromised if the Primary and Alternate channels have failed.

Compartmentation are the procedures and practices designed to ensure that each member of a clandestine organization knows only that which he needs to know about the personnel, structure, and activities of the rest of the organization. The purpose is to limit the damage to the organization, which can occur as a result of various forms of compromise.

CLANDESTINE COMMUNICATIONS:

Clandestine Communications

This is a basic term used in clandestine activity, which means operational contact between persons within the clandestine organization or the transmission of messages or data, and/or the transportation of supplies and equipments. It consists primarily of the adaptation of everyday communication techniques to the special requirements of the clandestine organization (use of telephone, face-to-face meetings, use of dead drops, and radio transmissions). Everyday communications techniques provide natural cover for any transmission. A survey of the Operational Area's normal social and commercial communication patterns are an essential part of the Case Operation planning process for that reason. Common social communication methods that have been adapted for clandestine communications are:

- Cell phones used to text open code or one-time pads
- Cell phones used to transmit information in cover conversations or transmitting photos where the subject of the photo is a coded message
- In some countries, satellite phones are used regularly and can be used in the same manner as described above
- Internet base phone service used in the above manner as well
- Internet chat rooms, forums, networking sites are obvious means of clandestine communication
- Placing classified ads in newspapers and internet sites
- Commercial delivery and courier services

In all communications with the Agent Handler, the Agent submits an Agents Report. The Agent's Report is a type of Intelligence Product/Report, which refers to an information report from agent or informant to its handler which maybe typewritten, handwritten, or verbal. It is transformed into another report before submission to higher headquarter.

Personal Meetings

This is a technique used when the above communication methods are unsatisfactory. Meetings are held for training purposes, to transmit intelligence reports, to transfer material, personnel, or cash, to plan an unforeseen mission, to lie up before exfiltration, and for agent testing. Meetings are held for purposes of internal communication; such cell meetings, or for external communications; such as meetings with the Agent Handler, or extreme circumstances, to meet with personnel from neutral or allied agencies.

Meetings are held between unacquainted personnel, acquainted personnel, or flash meetings: that is; brush meetings, agent or car tosses, and agent pickups. Flash meetings are brief encounters which may be between either personnel that are acquainted or unacquainted with each other. Brief or Flash meetings are utilized when the threat from opposition counterintelligence forces is extremely high.

Meetings are very useful for Agent Control. Because of this, meetings are usually held according to the following schedule:

- Scheduled
- Unscheduled
- Introductory or emergency

Scheduled meetings require the agent to be present at a meeting on a regular basis, usually weekly. This provides the Agent Handler with a perfect opportunity to monitor the agent through surveillance or questioning concerning past reports. It also tests the agent's reliability over a period of time. The scheduled meetings will have a fall back plan to meet at the same time on a different date at the same location.

Unscheduled meetings are used when information to be transmitted is too urgent to wait for the scheduled meeting. These types of meetings are also a method of surprise testing the agent. Unscheduled meetings are also used to reestablish lost contact with an agent. In this case, the Agent Handler usually is not present at the meeting site but rather arranges for surveillance of both the agent's route to the meeting and the meeting site itself to determine the presence of counterintelligence surveillance. The Agent Handler then determines whither or not to initiate contact with the agent.

The third category of meeting is either for initial contact with a potential agent or an emergency meeting usually to extract the agent from the operational area.

All meetings have in common the following steps, known as the Clandestine Action Cycle:

- Alert-the agent is alerted to the date and time of the meeting. The agent plans his cover for traveling to the meeting site
- Surveillance detection-the participants each follow Surveillance Detection Route to the meeting. This SDR will have at least three stops or points where opposition mobile and foot surveillance can be detected.
- Dry Cleaning-if surveillance is detected, the SDR will also include an area where the agent can break contact with opposition surveillance. This break can be momentary; to allow for a brush meeting or servicing a dead drop; or the agent may attempt to effect a break of longer duration. This is especially the

case when the agent needs to escape and evade, or for lengthy meetings such as debriefings at a safe house. If the agent intends to continue further operations, he should make sure the dry cleaning appears unintentional

- Operational activity-this can be any clandestine intelligence activity, from meetings to collection activities such as reconnaissance and surveillance.

- Dry Cleaning-at the completion of the operational activity, dry cleaning is once again utilized to insure a clean break from the site.

- SDR-during travel back to the station, surveillance detection routes are used with at least three stops to discover any efforts by opposition forces to track the operational personnel. If the safe site/safe house must remain undetected, then the cycle of dry cleaning and surveillance detection is utilized as many times as necessary

- Cover/housing-upon return, if necessary a cover story may used to explain the activities of the operational personnel during their absence.

The Operational Activity part of this cycle differs with each type of clandestine activity planned. What all meetings have in common are the use of Physical Signals and Verbal Signals. Physical Signal are signals that are placed in a person or to indicate safety or danger so as to recognize an individual. Verbal Signals use double-talk or countersigns to confirm they are talking to the right person. There are two kinds of physical signals; danger or safe signals and identification signals. Physical signals should be prominent or obvious enough to be seen and recognized at a distance, but they should not be out of the ordinary. Verbal signals are used primarily for recognition in meetings between two un-acquainted individuals. These signals should be in two stages: initial and confirmation. Initial recognition is given in the first part of the exchange and confirmation is given in a further unrelated exchange of sign and countersign. Physical signals are also placed by the first person scheduled to arrive at a meeting site to signal that the site is safe to approach.

Flash Meetings

Flash meetings are used in high risk areas where the agent may be under surveillance but must also transmit or receive materials or documents in order to satisfy the operational requirements. These meetings also use the Clandestine Action Cycle but have added elements besides physical signals or verbal signals and that is the Rendezvous Point which is a pre-arranged meeting at a given time and place, from which to begin an action.

The operational phase of Brush Meetings begins when both parties have arrived at the rendezvous point but are separated by a small distance. Simultaneously, both parties either turn or advance toward each other and at a position momentarily concealed from surveillance, the pass is made. Both parties then separately follow the Clandestine Action Cycle as they exit the area.

In car tosses and agent pickups, the rendezvous is between an individual and a motor vehicle. In this case, after the physical signals have been exchanged, both parties proceed towards each other at a pace which allows the operational activity to be completed. In the Car Toss, either the agent tosses an item into the motor vehicle or one of the occupants of the vehicle tosses something to the agent. During a Pickup, the agent enters the motor vehicle while the vehicle is momentarily concealed from surveillance. In Agent Drop Offs, obviously the reverse is true.

Safe Sites and Safe Houses

Safe sites and safe houses are categorized for planning and agent management purposes as follows:

- Unmanned and concealed-these are caves, shelters, cabins, certain types of motels or motor lodges, or isolated wooded clearings that are left unattended until needed
- Unmanned/maintained-these are apartments, houses or warehouses that are maintained by a Site Agent. Vacation cabins are an example of such a site.
- Manned/secret-a secret room of a home or business occupied by a Site Agent.
- Manned/assisted-these are dwellings with staff that provide services to the Agent

These locations have several common features; they are under the Agent Handler's control, they provide cover or concealment of clandestine activity, they have several secure approaches and exits, observation from the site is good, surveillance of the site is limited, as well as having no overt link to the agent or his employers.

Before use, these sites must surveyed by support personnel and primed. Safe houses and safe sites are primed with physical signals that indicate that the site is safe to approach. The Site Agent is responsible for setting safety and danger signals.

Cut-Out Device

Is a measure in Operational Security which promotes the avoidance of direct contact between personnel or units in intelligence organization which impede investigation by the active opposition be reducing the opportunity to observe direct contact. Cut-Out measures include:

- Dead drops
- Live drops (used seldom)
- Couriers
- Special email drop
- Mail forwarding addresses
- Caches

Cut-Outs are used most often in areas not under the Agent Handlers control and where opposition counterintelligence measures are effective. Dead drops and Live Drops utilize the same Clandestine Activity Cycle as personal meetings. Dead drop locations should also be concealed from direct observation. Certain locations, such as public restrooms, libraries, museums, and government and professional buildings lend themselves to use as dead drop sites. Certain areas of parks and rural roads also are good locations depending on the characteristics of the Operational Area.

Meeting sites and dead drop casing:

- Recon projected route to site at time site is planned to be utilized

- Recon exit route at time when site is planned to be utilized

- Note what dates and times site is available

- Note passive opposition (pedestrians, traffic patterns, etc.)

- Note active opposition (police, surveillance teams, etc.)

- Note possible observation sites of site

- Note if direct observation of any operational activity at site is possible

- Record details of site (map, sketches, photos, address, coordinates, description/type of neighborhood, etc.)

External Communication

Many times the agent handler is unable to directly communicate with the case officer, especially in the case of Resident Operations.   In these cases, a means of external communications is required.   Some effective examples of external communications are:

- Satellite phones-this equipment however, needs to be cached in a secure location to prevent compromise

- Email-stenography may be used in some cases to transmit complete documents but in technically advanced areas, open code should be the only type of messages sent by email

- International cell phones-code from one time pads are used in texting

- Radio-because of the advances in telecommunications, radios almost obsolete and must stored in the same manner as satellite phones

- International delivery services-messages can usually be sent securely and quickly using this type of communication channel. However, only open code should be used in this type of message

- Courier-documents may concealed on the courier and usually transmitted safely.

- Mail-the slowest and subject many interruptions in third world countries. This should be the last choice.

Codes are a system in which arbitrary group of symbols representing units of plain text of varying length such as symbols may constitute of syllables, words, phrases, or sentences. After any meeting, the Agent Handler must write a Contact report to document the circumstances of the meeting as well as observations and operational information that will not be added to other intelligence reports. The Agent Handler may issue a Spot Report according to the urgency of the information. Spot Reports are one-time reports used by all echelons to transmit intelligence or information of immediate value. Since the information or intelligence may have an immediate and significant impact on current planning and operations, speed of transmission of the spot report is essential.

Conclusion:

The Communication and Control is the very heart of Agent Operations. This part of the operation may take up the much of the planning process but is well worth it. The Communications Plan should include three parts: Continuity, Control, and Security.

Continuity is ensured by a redundant three channel system that includes a Primary Channel, an Alternate Channel, and a Emergency Channel. The Primary and Alternate Channels should emphasize security, while the Emergency requires speed and directness. Security is provided by utilizing normal social and commercial communications, as well as the judicious use of codes and ciphers.

Agent Control is the focus of the Communication Schedule. Scheduled, Non-Scheduled, and Emergency communications assist the Agent Handler in managing the Agent as well as assisting in the continuity of the information flow. In this manner both the safety of the agent and the security of the information are assured.

CHAPTER 14

AGENT DEBRIEFING

Debriefing Step in Operational Cycle

Once the agent comes back to the base of operations, he is taken or directed to the safe place for debriefing. Debriefing is the systematic withdrawal from the agent of all the information he has acquired, consciously or unconsciously, while on the mission. We must prepare for the debriefing thoroughly; the major items to be considered are: the operational plan on which the mission was based and the briefing record we have made prior to the agent's dispatch. He is requested to give a brief account of the mission and information obtained; this account serves as a debriefing guide for his chief. First information of PRIORITY ONE is discussed. The type of information is reported to higher headquarters on a priority basis in the form of a "spot report". Then the debriefing continues and the agent is interrogated in reference to the intelligence information he has. Here also, the information is derived from the agent in accordance with its priority and importance. After the agent has submitted all intelligence information, the operational debriefing is initiated. The agent is required to give a detailed account of his travel, obstacles encountered, roadblocks, and security measures observed.

Conclusion:

Every effort must made to extract as much information as possible from the agent. If the agent is in a location controlled by the Case Officer/Agent Handler, this debriefing may closely resemble an interrogation. During an operational meeting however, the debriefing also contains a large measure of moral building to fortify the agent before he returns to his mission.

CHAPTER 15

Payment Step in Operational Cycle

Payment to the Agent is one of the steps in the Operational Cycle wherein an intelligence organization must adhere to written agreements regulations and the local SOPs in question of payment. After this consideration, however, the mechanics of payment are very flexible. It is of importance for the staff to realize that no set amount of pay may be established for any type of information since this approach is unrealistic and may encourage operational dishonesty. The amount paid for the reports may differ radically from agent to agent area of residence of an agent; his pay may differ radically from the pay of other agents with similar targets. The method of payments may also differ greatly. Some may be paid on a production basis, or they may be paid on a monthly basis. No matter by what means of payment is affected, it is imperative for the chief to keep exact records on expenditures. This is, of course, not a question of trust in the principles, since this information will play an important part in subsequent analysis of the operation. In this connection, it is important for the staff to realize that the expectation of immediate results for funds extended is an unrealistic point of view. The launching of an operation may sometimes take months and a large monetary investment, before it starts producing a product. Certain operations of consider quantity of reports above quality.

Conclusion:

Payment to an agent during an operation sometimes requires subtle management skills. Care must be taken to protect the agent from displaying suspicious affluence. In many third world operational environments, currency is not as useful as material goods. In these cases, it is important to assess what the agent needs and be able to deliver it. It may be that an equal equivalent must be determined in order to satisfy the agent's contractual agreements.

CHAPTER 16

Disposition Step in Operational Cycle

After the agent has been debriefed and paid, the chief must decide on his future disposition. In some cases the agent may be re-dispatched immediately. Fragmentary information elicited during the debriefing may convince the chief that the agent requires additional training in some fields. Doubtful information that the agent contributed during the debriefing may require additional operational testing of the agent. Some cases, especially after hazardous mission or possible compromise of the agent within the certain target area, may require that he be given a period of rest within the base area. In some cases, compromise is obvious, when the agent has displayed inefficiently or derogatory character traits, or if the agent was used on one-time basis only, termination of employment may be deemed appropriate. The method of termination of employment and any difficulties connected with it must be planned for during the initial recruiting phase of the agent. In other words, even if he possesses all the necessary qualifications for recruitment, but it is obvious to the recruiter that termination of this individual would be difficult and may cause embarrassment to the intelligence effort, no recruitment attempt may be made.

Termination

Termination is the severance of a relationship between an agent and the clandestine organization. If possible, this should be done in such a way as to preserve the long-term security and viability of the organization, the facts concerning the agent's relationship to the organization, and any future clandestine usefulness the agent might have.

Conclusion:

Disposition and Termination are steps which must considered before recruitment of the agent. In Case Operation Planning, termination must be considered an essential factor in Operational Security. In operations of extreme sensitivity, the terminated agent should be monitored for several years after the operation. This monitoring may include polygraph testing to determine if the terminated agent is guilty of security breaches.

CHAPTER 17

REPORTING

Reporting Step in Operational Cycle

Information delivered by the agent is written in the information report that is the answer to the original requirements levied on the intelligence unit, is the most important single element. It is the reason for existence of the organ as a whole and it is the final product of all of your efforts. For this reason it must meet certain standards. It must answer the requirements as completely as possible. It must be clear, and accurate, and most important of all, it must be timely. Other reports, specifically Operational Reports, must also be completed. It is these operational reports, which are forwarded to the Research and Analysis Branch, which are of primary importance for and a repository of information of great assistance to any future planning of operations of similar nature. These operational reports do not contain any information in answer to requirements but rather describe the ways and means that this information was collected and any difficulties, which the agent encountered during his mission. They also present a chronological history of any given operation, which assists the staff in determining compliance with regulations.

An Information Report is an Intelligence Product, which refers to any report written and submitted immediately after obtaining the required information derived from approved projects.

Intelligence Information Reporting is the process of recording in prescribed format and transmitting the raw materials collected in response to collection requirements.

An Information Report is an Intelligence Product, which refers to any report written and submitted immediately after obtaining the required information derived from approved projects.

Agent's Report

The Agent's Report is a type of Intelligence Product/Report, which refers to a supervisory report from agent or informant to its handler maybe typewritten or handwritten. It is transformed into another report before submission to higher headquarter.

Conclusion:

The Reporting Step is where the Operation Cycle reenters the Intelligence Cycle. These reports are then subject to processing like all other sources of intelligence and are then disseminated to the intelligence customer.

Part III

APPENDICES

APPENDIX A

Definition of Terms

Action Agent - a recruited and documented intelligence agent with access and/or placement in a threat target.

Agent - a person who is aware that he is engaged in a clandestine activity

on behalf of a sponsor and who submits to some degree of control by the clandestine organization

Agent Access - the ability of the action agent to obtain information relative to his /her assignment or position on target personalities/organization.

    a.   Excellent Access - an Action Agent is considered to have excellent access to a particular area/field of a target organization or on target personalities if the reports/information he/she provided are evaluated or characterized to have fo-cus/concentration, regularity and continuity.

b. Moderate Access - an Action Agent is considered to have moderate access to a particular target if the information provided by him/her is evaluated or characte-rized to have either of the following: with concentration, regularity and lesser degree of continuity, with concentration, continuity, and lesser degree of regu-larity; and, with concentration, lesser, degree of regularity and continuity, than that of an Action Agent with excellent access c. Limited Access   -   an Agent Action is considered to have limited access on a particular area/field/target personality when he cannot or is not expected to concentrate his report in a particular field/area/target personality, no regularity and no continui-ty.

Agent Acquisition - the process by which potential agents are located, their suitability determined, and their eventual recruitment into the clandestine organization

Agent Handler - an organic member of an intelligence unit who supervises and manages the activities of action agents to enhance the success of a case operation

Agent Handling - the supervision and management of the agent and his activities so as to minimize potentially dangerous effects of personal and professional problems and en-hance the likelihood of success in the clandestine undertaking

Agent Placement - the position occupied by the action agent or informant/action agent in the target organizations.

Assessment - the analysis of the motivation and qualifications of an agent candidate to determine his suitability for the susceptibility to recruitment

Briefing - Preparation of a person for a specific mission by describing the objective, the requirements, and the situation he is expected to encounter, and the methods he is to employ

Case Officer - officers directly in-charge of running a case operation.

Case Operation - a definite target specific activity conducted in relation to an intelligence project under which it is affected. Several case operations may fall under one intelligence project.

Compartmentation - procedures and practices designed to ensure that each member of a clandestine organization knows only that which he needs to know about the personnel, structure, and activities of the rest of the organization. The purpose is to limit the damage to the organization, which can occur as a result of various forms of compromise.

Control - forms of influence used to induce an agent to accept more readily the direction and discipline of the clandestine organization

Debriefing - detailed questioning of an agent (or of a person who has been involved in a situation of intelligence or operational interest and who is aware of the questioner's interest in intelligence matters) for the purpose of acquiring as accurate and complete coverage as possible of all matter of operational or intelligence concern

Development - the relatively long term cultivation of a relationship between a member of the clandestine organization and potential agent with a view toward investigation, assessment, and eventual recruitment of the candidate.

Environment - the setting in which a clandestine activity takes place

Intelligence Funds - funds for purchase of information such as payment of informant/action agents, incentives, transportation, meals, billeting, representation expenses, and other incidentals. Details and supporting papers are kept in the custody of the Project Officer until such time the project is declassified and ready for audit. This differentiates the discretionary expenses from other object classes of intelligence MOE.

Intelligence MOE - the budget for the maintenance and operation of the discretionary expenses, which are technically known as unit's intelligence functions and activities. It includes funds for confidential/intelligence funds.

Intelligence Project - a project proposal that has been approved by proper authorities

Intelligence Project Management - is the identification of specific functions and the determining specific responsibilities in the various stages of an intelligence operation

Interviewing - gathering information through conversation with a person

who knows that he is giving wanted information but is not aware of the clandestine sponsor, connections, and purpose of the interviewer

Investigation - the activities undertaken to accumulate of substantiate hard facts about a potential agent. In a broader sense, and outside

the framework of Agent Acquisition, the term can be applied to the accumulation of facts about any agents

Operational Expenses - expenses incurred in pursuit of Case Operation

objectives such as follow-up if leads/information, limited investigation, casing, surveillance, counter-action operations, photography, tape recording and other related operational matters.

Principal Agent - an intelligence agent who has developed his information net within a target threat group or in a particular area of operation.

Project officer - an officer directly in-charge of running an intelligence project.

Project Proposal - a recommended general intelligence plan of action to address a throat target by infiltration and penetration and the like, for the purpose of neutralization or defeating that threat group through

the acquisition of timely and accurate intelligence on the threat group's capabilities, vulnerabilities, and intentions.

Recruitment - the act of inducing an agent candidate to enter into a clandestine relationship on behalf of a sponsor and to accept some degree of direction and control by the clandestine organization

Requirement -descriptions, varying in detail and specification of information needed or results desired by a sponsor and assigned to a clandestine organization for action

Spotting - the systematic search for potential assets; especially the acquisition and recording of information which will assist in

determining an individual's suitability, susceptibility and operational usefulness

Support Agent - a person who extends assistance to the intelligence operation

Target - the person, place, thing or action against which clandestine activity is directed

Termination - severance of a relationship between an agent and the clandestine organization.   If possible, this should be done in such a way as to preserve the long-term security and viability of the organization, the facts concerning the agent's relationship to the organization, and any future clandestine usefulness the agent might have

Threat target - any group of persons, organization, installation, or activity considered inimical to national interest and security and is the objective of an intelligence project.

APPENDIX B

A Typical Intelligence Agency Hierarchy

Intelligence agency - a unit responsible for gathering and interpreting information about an enemy

Intelligence directorate- one of the major components of an intelligence agency- (Intelligence Analysis, Secret Intelligence, Science and Technology, Support for example) The entire staff of a such a bureau or department.

Intelligence group- An administrative unit of directorate personnel or intelligence activities gathered or located together by similar geographical responsibilities and identical intelligence products (Near Eastern and South Asian Analysis)

Intelligence division - a specialized administrative division of a large intelligence directorate (counters intelligence, counter terrorism)

Intelligence Office- an administrative department of an intelligence division dealing with particular activity or function.

Intelligence Desk-An administrative department of a large intelligence office in charge of a specified operation or geographical area

Intelligence Station-field operations center where staff is involved in intelligence activities in specific AO

Sub Station-component of operations center involved in specific intelligence activity or responsible for section of AO

APPENDIX C

Intelligence Unit Command Structure and Duties

The Project Officer is the officer directly in-charge of running an intelligence project. An Intelligence Project is a project geared towards providing intensive intelligence coverage of targets thru the direct and indirect infiltration of Action Agents or Penetration Agents into the rank and file of the enemy organization. The particular intelligence activity is funded through a specially allocated intelligence fund for "asset development program" and use mainly to finance the salary of the recruited; Penetration Agents and operational allowance of the Agent Handler, Support Agent and Project Officer.

The Project Officer's administrative responsibilities include creating, maintaining, and updating the project database; liaison with other involved agencies, and overall mission planning. The Project Officer manages all Intelligence Funds for the purchase of information such as payment of informants, incentives, transportations, meals, billeting, representation expenses and other incidentals. Details and supporting papers are kept in the custody of the project officer until, such time the project be classified and ready for audit. The Project Officer also is responsible for the Intelligence MOE,that is, the budget for the maintenance and operation of discretionary expenses, which are technically known as the unit's intelligence functions and activities. It includes funds for confidential/intelligence funds. The Project Officer conducts overall project management through the identification of specific functions and the determining of specific responsibilities in the various stages of an intelligence operation.

The Case Officer in intelligence parlance refers to an officer directly in-charge of running an intelligence case operation. A Case Operation is a definite target specific activity conducted in relation to an intelligence project under which it is affected. Several case operations may fall under one intelligence project. The Case Officer is responsible for the Case Operation Plan, a plan of action on the specific targets covering a specific period within which neutralization of target or threat activity is affected. The Case Officer recruits and controls agents through the Agent Handler. The Case Officer is responsible for documenting and is accountable for Operational Expenses, such as expenses incurred in the of Case Operation objectives such as follow up of leads/information, limited investigation, casing, surveillance, counter-action operations, photography, tape recording, and other related operational matters.

Agent Handler is a term in Agent Acquisition, which refers to an organic member of an intelligence unit who supervises and manages the activities of action agents to enhance the success of case operation. In overseas operations, Agent Handlers are also known as

Access Agents because they are native personnel who have access to population groups with access to required information. Access Agents should be chosen from those individuals who have a history of long association with intelligence personnel. They should be individuals who are employed in a position of trust such as translators, secretaries, host nation training cadre, liaison, or advisory counterparts. The Agent Handler is responsible for evaluating Agent Reports , a type of Intelligence Product/Report, which refers to a supervisory report from agent or informant to its handler maybe typewritten or handwritten. It is transformed into another report before submission to higher headquarter.

TYPES OF AGENTS

Agent is a person who is aware that he is engaged in a clandestine activity on behalf of a sponsor and who submits to some degree of control by the clandestine organization.

Access Agents- are native personnel who have access to population groups with access to required information.

Recruited Informants/Action Agents-Informants are individuals who obtain the required information during the course of their normal daily activities. They are distinguished from casual informants because they submit to operational control. Informant/Action Agents, sometimes known as Low Level Sources, are primarily used for area intelligence. Hotel and restaurant personnel, merchants in bazaars, traveling businessmen are examples of Recruited informants.

Principal Agent - an intelligence agent who has developed his information net within a target group or in a particular area of operations.

Resident Agent-is a term for an agent who is the resident of a third country while performing the duties of an Agent Handler for operations in the target country.

Action Agent – a term used in Agent Acquisition, which refers to a recruited and documented intelligence agent with access and or placement to a threat group.

Penetration Agent-a term used in Agent Acquisition, which refers to a recruited and documented agent with placement and access in a threat group. They may be recruited outside the target and placed therein or more usually recruited from personnel within the target itself. Penetration Agents are particularly vulnerable to detection and must receive intensive security instruction to prevent their compromise.

Site Agent-in Agent Acquisition, an agent in-charge of the security survey and security measures at a certain location to be visited by the principal.

Support Agent a person who extends assistance to the intelligence operations.

An Intelligence Project may consist of many target specific activities managed by one or several Case Officers depending on the complexity of the project. Each Case Officer will head a team of several Agent Handlers. The number of Agent Handlers assigned to each Case Officer will vary according several factors, including target hardness, cultural factors, and other risk factors. Each Agent Handler may have a few or several Agents reporting to him depending on the organization of the network itself.

TYPES OF AGENT NETS

An Individual network is a type of informant network which is composed of an unlimited number of individual informants controlled by and reporting directly to the Agent Handler. This type of net provides the greatest amount of control, but limits security of operation and coverage. This type of net is the quickest to set up, limited only by the Agent Handler's access to the Source Population. This type of intelligence network is often utilized in short term undercover operations.

Principal Agent Net is a type of agent network that comprises a Principal Agent and sub-agents. Control over the sub-agents is exercised through the Principal and not direct. However, the Agent Handler must know the identity, location, and other pertinent data about the sub-agent (provided by principal agent to Agent Handler). There is more security in this type of net since the Agent Handler has been exposed to only one person, the Principal Agent. This network is also known as Intelligence Cell organization. The cell consists of no more than four members, the Cell Leader, also referred to as the Principal Agent, and three Action Agents. The Action Agents are not known to each other as agents and never meet as such. If the cell grows with additional recruits, a trusted member of the cell takes over as Principal Agent in most cases.

A Mixed Network is a type of Agent Network, which is composed of both an Individual net and Principal Agent net. It is designed to give maximum coverage and yet maintain the necessary security. The two (2) mixed types of net can be used on separate targets or individual agents may be placed on the targets covered by the Principal Agent net for purposes of supplementing and/or double-checking the information supplied by the Principal Agent net.

APPENDIX D

PLANS AND REPORT FORMATS

INFORMATION REQUIREMENT FORM

DATE:_____

STATION NO. :____

FROM: (SECTION OF) STATION

TO: (COLLECTION UNIT)

PRECEDENCE: (ROUTINE) (PRIORITY) (IMMEDIATE)

BACKGROUND: (GIVE A DESCRIPTION OF THE SITUATION AND/OR FACT OR THE REASON FOR LEVYING A REQUIREMENT)

REQUIREMENTS: (STATE WHAT INFORMATION IS REQUIRED THAT SHOULD BE REALISTICALLY WITHIN THE CAPABILITIES OF THE TASKED AGENCY)

RECOMMENDED MEASURES: (BASED ON KNOWLEDGE AND ABILITIES OF SOURCES OR UNITS AVAILABLE TO AGENCY, SUGGEST WHICH MEASURES APPEAR BEST CAPABLE OF FULFILLING THE REQUIREMENT)

ANSWER REQUESTED BY: (FULL NAME AND POSITION)

PROJECT PROPOSAL FORMAT

SUBJECT:_____

DATE___/___/___:

PROJECT PLAN NO____.

1. PURPOSE:

2. ASSUMPTIONS/SITUATION :

    a.   Pertinent information from Target Study and Target Area Study

        i.   Geographical Areas

       ii.   Population demographics

           1.   economic

           2.   social

           3.   political

           4.   national

           5.   religious

           6.   subversive

    7. criminal

  iii. Popular opinions and group attitudes

    1. of groups toward each other

    2. of groups toward external threats

  iv. Key individuals

    1. political leaders

    2. social/religious leaders

    3. business leaders

  v. Opposition counterintelligence forces

    1. organization

    2. methods of operation

3. ORGANIZATIONAL CONCEPT:

  a. Where and how to organize Humint operations

    i. Potential agent groups

    ii. Potential agent locations

4. ORGANIZATION OF AGENT NETWORKS

  a. According to geographical areas

  b. According to demographic groupings

  c. Focusing on target's functions or activities

    d.   Focus on specific individuals

5.   SECTION PLANNING

    a.   Operational Sections

         i.   Technical intelligence

        ii.   Surveillance and reconnaissance

      iii.   Intelligence

      iv.   Communication

    b.   Support Sections

         i.   Logistics

        ii.   Security

      iii.   Transportation

      iv.   Purchasing, caches

       v.   Fabrication and technical support

      vi.   Public Relations

     vii.   Administrative

6.   STAFF

    a.   Expected staff requirements

7. MAINTAINENCE AND OPERATIONAL EXPENSES

CASE OPERATION PLAN

SUBJECT: DATE:

REPORT NO.

PROJECT NO.

REFERENCES:

1. MISSION:

    a.   Requirement:

    b.   Objective:

    c.   Base of Operations:

2. PERSONEL:

    a.   Confidential Source Personnel:

    b.   Staff Personnel:

        i.   Intelligence Project Officer:

        ii.   Intelligence Project Case Officer:

        iii.   Alternate Intelligence Project Case Officer:

        iv.   Project Liaison Officer:

        v.   Alternate Project Liaison Officer:

3.   COVER AND DOCUMENTATION:

4.   EXECUTION:

    a.   Concept of Operations:

        i.   (Type of operation and coverage,overt and covert)

        ii.   (Focus of target coverage, limits of operation)

        iii.   (Point of contact with other agencies)

        iv.   (Specific EEI)

    b.   Target List

        i.   (Target nations)

        ii.   (Target Organizations)

        iii.   (Target Activities)

        iv.   (Target individuals of influence or interest)

    c.   Implementation:

        i.   Overt Phase:(Staff responsible for liaison, overt collection, spotting and accessing)

        ii.   Covert Phase: (Staff responsible for vetting, recruitment, targeting, training, control, and disposition of agents)

5.   COMMUNICATION:

    a.   Staff Communications:

    b.   Primary Scheduled Agent Communication:

    c.   Alternate Non-Scheduled Agent Communication:

    d.   Emergency/Alert Agent Communication:

6.   TRAINING

    a.   Security

          i.   Operational Security

          ii. Personal Security

   b. Cover

          i.   Status

          ii. Action

   c. Communications

   d. Mission Specific Training

7. FINANCE AND LOGISTICS:

   a. Diplomatic pouch

   b. Host country financed

   c. Financed through organizational cover

   d. Financed through Criminal activity

8. TECHNICAL SUPPORT:

9. TERMINATION:

   a. Causes for Termination:

   b. Commitments for Reimbursement:

   c. Knowledgeability of Agent: (limits)

          i.   Code name, cover for action, cover for status, and physical description of Control and Alternate Control Officer

          ii. Location of meeting sites

          iii. Means of alternate and emergency contact methods

          iv. Approach method used by Control Officer in initial contact with source

   d. Non disclosure statement:

   e. Security Considerations:

10. COORDINATION AND LIAISON:(Staff responsible for Liaison with agencies sharing AO responsibility)

11. REPORTING AND ADMINISTRATION:

    a.   Operational Reports

    b.   Agent Reports

12. ADDITIONAL SUPPORT REQUIREMENTS:

13. POINT OF CONTACT:

Annex A-Cover and Documentation

1. Operational security and cover

2. Cover for Staff

3. Agent cover

4. Documentation

    a.   Staff

    b.   Agent

Annex B-Communications

1. Primary

2. Alternate

3. Emergency

Annex C-Finance and Logistics

Annex D-Termination

2. Termination of Operation:

3. Termination of Agent with Prejudice:

4. Termination of Agent without Prejudice:

5. Commitments:

6. Knowledgeability: (Agent)

    a. Knowledge of Personnel

    b. Knowledge of Modus Operandi

Annex E-Security Considerations

1. (Risk of Intelligence activities compromising operation)

    a. (Social, Employment, Familial compromise of agent, and counter measures)(Training in personal security and operations security)

    b. (Law enforcement, Security compromise of Control Officer/agent and counter measures)(Training in operations security)

2. (Procedure followed if compromise occurs)

    a. Organizational damage control

    b. Source security and evacuation

3. Standards for Security

    a. Need to Know-Knowledgeability list

    b. Other parties that may be granted Need to Know at later date

Annex F-Knowledgeability List

SOURCE DATA SUMMARY FORMAT

1. NAME:

2. DATE OF BIRTH:

3. CURRENT ADDRESS:

4. PLACE OF BIRTH:

5. EMPLOYMENT-INCOME:

6. PAST EMPLOYMENT:

7. EDUCATION:

8. MILITARY TRAINING AND SPECIALTIES:

9. RANK AND SSN AND UNITS:

10. PREVIOUS PLACES OF RESIDENCE:

11. AREAS AND CITIES WHERE TRAVELED:

12. FAMILY:

    a. WIFE:

    b. CHILDREN:

    c. LOCATION:

    d. HEALTH:

    e. NATIONALITY:

    f. EMPLOYED:

    g. SOCIAL STATUS:

13. RELIGIOUS BACKGROUND:

14. POLICE RECORD:

15. PERSONALITY APPRAISAL:

SPOTTING REPORT FORMAT:

1. Initial Contact

- When, where and how was the potential source spotted?

- Deliberate contact or accidental contact?

- Who initiated contact-Source? Or Spotter?

- List of those at initial contact

2. Follow up Contacts

- Circumstances of follow up meetings

- Frequency of meetings

- Dates of meetings

- Meetings arraigned or accidental?

- Pretext used for arraigned meetings

- Who arraigned meetings?

- Who observed meetings?

3. Approach used and nature of relationship\

- Approach used to initiate contact

- Nature of relationship with contact

- Any observed changes in contact attitude or behavior?

- Personality type

- Character traits

- Motivation?

- Potential for development of contact

- Approaches indicated

Name Trace and Investigation initiated?

Approved

Not Approved

CONTACT REPORT FORMAT

Agent Handler is required to submit contact report after every contact with Agent

SOURCE (S):

DATE:

TIME:

LOCATION:

AGENT HANDLER:

AGENT EVALUATION:

CONTENT EVALUATION:

REPORTED INFORMATION:

ROUTE/TRANSPORTATION USED:

      A.   AGENT:

      B.   AGENT HANDLER:

CONTACT SECURITY PROCEDURES:

INFORMATION LEADS:

NEW PIR ASSIGNED TO AGENT:

NEW AGENT PERSONNAL DATA:

COMMENTS:

AGENT REGISTRATION CARD FORMAT:

Personal data

Photo

Biography

Military/political history

Habits hobbies and idiosyncrasies

Date and circumstances of first contact

Frequency places and types of contact

Identities of all personnel involved

Target and access of source

Type amount and method of payment

Source's current evaluation

Source's real name and name of substitute

Agent registration cards are kept on file in a secure location separate from the Agent Dossier File. Registration cards serve as a quick reference for asset availability during case operation planning.

OPERATIONAL RECONNAISSANCE REPORT

1. Location

    a. Coordinates

    b. Address

2. Description

    a. Rural

        i.   Geographical features

        ii. Population information

             1. demographics

             2. density

    b. urban

        i.   building characteristics

        ii. population information

             1. demographics

        iii. traffic patterns

3. Available Dates and Times

4. Available Seasons

5. Routes to Site

    a. Primary Route

    b. Secondary Route

        c.   Escape and Evasion Route

6.   Security Considerations

        a.   Active opposition

            i.   Counterintelligence, police, paramilitary, insurgent forces

            ii.   Criminal elements

        b.   Passive opposition

            i.   Traffic patterns

            ii.   Pedestrian patterns

7.   Date of Reconnaissance

8.   Area Maps/Sketches/Photos of Site

MEETING PLAN

1. Purpose of Meeting

2. Date/Time

3. General Location

4. Specific Location

5. Contact Procedures (Can be used for Agent Pickup also)

    a. Procedure (example: Route to Meeting)

    b. Procedure (example: Description of Meeting)

    c. Procedure (example: Counter Surveillance Check)

6. Recognition Signals

    a. Visual (far signal)

    b. Verbal (close signal)

7. Danger Signal

8. Cover

    a. Cover for Status of participants

    b. Cover for Action

9. Security Considerations

10. Alternate Contact

11. Instructions to Insure Continuity

12. Props Required

13. Area Maps/Sketches

DEAD DROP PLAN

1. Location

2. Description

3. Drop Site

4. Specific Drop Location

5. Size and Type of Container

6. Servicing Time

7. Cover

8. Route to Drop

9. Seasonal Limitations

10. Security Considerations

11. Props Required

12. Date of Casing

13. Cased by: CODE NAME

14. Load Signal

15. Unload Signal

16. Area Maps/Sketches

INTELLIGENCE INFORMATION REPORT

(ORIGINATING) STATION

I HEADINGS:

- REPORT #
- DATE:
- # OF PAGES:
- TO:
- ORIGINATING AGENCY: (1)
- AREA: (2)
- SUBJECT: (3)
- DATE OF INFORMATION: (4)
- DATE AND PLACE OF ACQUISITION: (5)
- SOURCE: (6)
- EVALUATION: (7)

II CONTENT:

III STATION COMMENTS:

NOTES:

1. Name of agency which provided information

2. Where the event took place

3. The subject of the report

4. When the event took place

5. When and where the originating agency obtained the information

6. Category of source: S-sigint report, U-penetration agent/informant, V- Allied troops, W- interrogation of EPW, X- government civilian employee, Y- general populace, Z-documents

7. Evaluation of the information made by the originating agency: (Source Evaluation) A-completely reliable, B-Usually reliable, C-Fairly reliable, D-Not usually reliable, E-Unreliable, F-Reliability cannot be judged (Information Evaluation) 1-Confirmed by other sources, 2-Probably true, 3-Possibly true, 4-Doubtfully true, 5-Improbable, 6-Truth cannot be judged

Appendix:

AGENT EVALUATION REPORT FORMAT

1. FULL NAME AND ADDRESS

2. DATE AND PLACE OF BIRTH

3. PRESENT ADDRESS

4. PLACEMENT/MISSION AND ASSIGNED CODE NAME

5. EVALUATION

6. ADDITIONAL INFORMATION

MONTHLY OPERATIONAL REPORT FORMAT

1. (CLASSIFICATION) PROJECT CODENAME

    a. Location:

    b. Confidential Sources utilized: (number of sources used)

    c. Information obtained through other sources (open sources, other agencies, etc.)

    d. Significant information obtained during period (give beginning date, ending date)

        i.   Source no. 1

        ii. Source no. 2, etc

    e. Operational status (significant developments in operation)

        i.   Development no.1

        ii. Development no. 2, etc

    f. Comments (operation ongoing)

    g. Recommendations (continue or terminate)

Appendix

Quarterly Progress Report Format

Unit

Station

Date:

Quarterly Progress Report

Period: Through:

Subject: (Name of Operation)

1. Circumstances: (Describe meetings, briefings, etc., and subjects discussed)

    a.

    b.

    c.

2. Recapitulation of Operational Progress during the Period: (Describe Operational details; Liaison meetings, agent meetings, continued Spotting and Assessment, etc.)

    a.

    b.

3. Significant Intelligence Information Developed: (list number of reports, against number of targets, and summary of information received)

  a.

  b.

4. Comments, Remarks, Recommendations:

  a.

  b.

Signature of Project Officer:

ADMINISTRATION FILES:

OPERATIONS PLAN FILES

Mission Analysis Report

Target Analysis Report

Target Area Study Report

Collection/Case Operation Plan

Target File

AGENT DOCUMENTATION FILE

1. Registration card or Agent's personal history statement

2. Agent contract

3. Codename agreement

4. Oath of Loyalty

5. Source Data Summary

6. Source control Data

7. Spotting and Recruitment Report

8. Operational testing Report

18097641R00130

Made in the USA
Lexington, KY
14 October 2012